Reading, Writing, and Talking Gender in Literacy Learning

Reading, Writing, and Talking Gender in Literacy Learning

Barbara J. Guzzetti
Josephine Peyton Young
Margaret M. Gritsavage
Laurie M. Fyfe
Arizona State University
Tempe, Arizona, USA

Marie Hardenbrook
Vanderbilt University
Nashville, Tennessee, USA

INTERNATIONAL
Reading
Association

800 Barksdale Road,
PO Box 8139
Newark, Delaware 19714-8139, USA
www.reading.org

NATIONAL READING CONFERENCE

National Reading Conference
122 South Michigan Avenue
Suite 1100
Chicago, Illinois 60603, USA

Director of Publications   Joan M. Irwin
Editorial Director, Books and Special Projects   Matthew W. Baker
Senior Editor, Books and Special Projects   Tori Mello Bachman
Permissions Editor   Janet S. Parrack
Production Editor   Shannon Benner
Assistant Editor   Corinne M. Mooney
Editorial Assistant   Tyanna L. Collins
Publications Manager   Beth Doughty
Production Department Manager   Iona Sauscermen
Supervisor, Electronic Publishing   Anette Schütz
Senior Electronic Publishing Specialist   Cheryl J. Strum
Electronic Publishing Specialist   R. Lynn Harrison
Proofreader   Charlene M. Nichols

Project Editor   Janet S. Parrack

Library of Congress Cataloging-in-Publication Data
    Reading, writing, and talking gender in literacy learning / Barbara J. Guzzetti . . . [et al.].
      p.   cm.— (Literacy studies series)
    Includes bibliographical references and index.
    1. Sex differences in education.   2. Sexism in education.   3. Language arts—Social aspects. I. Guzzetti, Barbara J. II. Series.
LC212.9.R4   2002   2001008578
302.2'244—dc21
ISBN 0-87207-300-9 (alk. paper)

To our colleagues and students from whom we have learned so much.

This review was supported by a Nila Banton Smith Research Dissemination Grant from the International Reading Association. The views expressed here are those of the authors and do not necessarily represent the views of the International Reading Association. The authors express their appreciation to Advisory Council members Donna Alvermann of the University of Georgia, Patricia Anders of the University of Arizona, and Carole Edelsky of Arizona State University.

Contents

Note From the Series Editors

In Australian young adult author John Marsden's novel *Winter* (2000), the main character, a 16-year-old girl named "Winter" returns to her former home. Her parents have been dead for 12 years and the rural property has been placed in a trust in her name. The house and surrounding acreage occupy a large wooded area in the hills. She finds the property is under the care of two crooks, illegally logging the surrounding forest, killing endangered wildlife, and siphoning funds from her trust. Winter, a bright, strong-willed young woman, takes on the emotionally draining task of firing the caretakers and renovating her parents' former home while researching the truth about her mother's death. "I was so tired I didn't think about being alone on the property: 16 years old and just me, on 600 hectares of farmland and bush" (Marsden, 2000, p. 89). This is a powerful story that disrupts gender stereotypes, particularly within the genre of young adult literature where women's voices are often echoes in the background or silenced entirely.

There is little doubt that the topic of gender and literacy learning has captured the interest of researchers from diverse areas including feminist scholarship, masculine theory, and critical theory. In particular, researchers have examined the role of reading and writing in a postmodern world where an unstable economic future often intersects with older, gender-based and social-class stereotypes. These limiting views of male and female identity endure at a time when we can least afford to limit students' flexibility in their identity construction. Postmodern globalization has replaced the anchor of stable factory employment with fluidity, destabilizing families, and rupturing identities. In Markus Zusak's novel *Fighting Ruben Wolfe* (2000), two young men help their family survive their dad's job loss as a plumber by boxing in an illegal gambling operation. "When your old man is eaten by his own shadow, you realize that maybe in every house, something so savage and sad and brilliant is standing up, without the world even seeing it" (Zusak, 2000, p. 32). When the two brothers settle down at night in their room to talk before going to sleep, their discourse departs from the tough male exteriors of the high school and boxing arena, and the print style changes to mark how sensitive they really are. Masculine theory offers a counterpoint lens for critically examining how boys are often stereotyped and how we keep reproducing these limited views of male identity.

Poststructural feminist scholars challenge essentialist notions of femininity. For example, literature offers a unique space where a reader may be transformed by identification with a character. Static roles based on gender are disrupted and a world of possible identity choices emerges. For example, Helen Harper, a critical feminist scholar, explored adolescent girls' complex and often contradictory responses to avant-garde feminist writing. She noted that this is "work committed to social transformation, namely to improve women's lives by seeking to understand the discursive formation of gendered identity" (Harper, 2000, p. 38).

In the past, it has been a daunting task for the scholar interested in gaining insights into contemporary research on gender and literacy. This work is scattered across a broad landscape of journals, books, dissertations, and monographs. The seventh book in the Literacy Studies Series, *Reading, Writing, and Talking Gender in Literacy Learning* provides a carefully crafted synthesis of research. The cumulative impact of this work will be realized when we challenge discourse that marginalizes people based on simplistic gender stereotypes and narrow views of identity. In the authors' words: "We also believe that it is important to offer students opportunities to explore gendered identities in and through reading, writing, and discussion, and to deconstruct the categories of male and female." We are indeed pleased to welcome readers to this new addition to the Series.

Thomas W. Bean
University of Nevada, Las Vegas
Las Vegas, Nevada, USA

Lisa Patel Stevens
State Department of Education
Honolulu, Hawaii, USA

Series Editors

References

Harper, H.J. (2000). *Wild words/dangerous desires: High school girls & feminist avant-garde writing.* New York: Peter Lang.
Marsden, J. (2000). *Winter.* Sydney: Macmillan.
Zusak, M. (2000). *Fighting Ruben Wolfe.* New York: Scholastic.

Review Board

CHAPTER 1

Our Stories, Our Intentions, and Our Methods: An Introduction

As European American, middle-class women and as researchers, we have observed how gender is produced and constructed in our lives and through our literacy practices. We have also seen how the power of social context influences literacy along stereotypical gender (or "gendered") lines. Our investigations in classrooms as university researchers and teacher researchers led us to attempt to make sense of those experiences in light of others' research and, consequently, to write this review of the literature on gender and literacies.

Our conversations with each other about our experiences and investigations showed us how gender affects students' literacy development and participation at all grade levels. For example, Barbara Guzzetti's (1996a, 1996b, 2001) research in high school science classes documented language patterns that marginalized females in their activity and talk about that activity in whole-class and small-group discussions. Barbara spent 2 years observing daily three sections of physics and honors physics classes composed of juniors and seniors who were college bound. She also spent a year observing freshmen in physical science, who were not college bound. Together with the physics teacher, Wayne Williams, and with some direction from his female students, Barbara documented discourse patterns the young men in these classes used to their advantage. These language patterns included interruptions, gaze aversion, and competitively gaining and holding the conversational floor, behaviors documented by researchers in other countries as well (see Tromel-Plotz, 1985, for a description of her observations in Denmark, or Cherland, 1994, for a report of her observations in Canada). Barbara and Wayne attempted to disrupt these gendered practices by grouping by gender for small-group labs, which did result in more symmetrical participation for females.

Barbara's observations in these science classes gave her the impetus to develop and offer a new graduate seminar class—Gender, Culture and Literacy—designed to raise awareness of how gender and culture affect literacy development and practice. In this course, participants reflected on their own gendered literacy practices in light of insights gained from class readings and discussions. A student in the first section of this class, Margaret Gritsavage (1997a), conducted an analysis of fellow graduate students' talk in class sessions. An analysis of the discourse of classroom talk showed that as Barbara as instructor intentionally gave up that role to become a coparticipant and facilitator, the relinquished power was taken up by the oldest male student in the class, Carl. Analysis of audiorecorded conversations from each session revealed how Carl dominated classroom discussions. He accomplished this with an asymmetrical number of conversational turns and the inordinate length of these turns, as well as by using interruptions to gain and maintain control of the conversational floor.

Another professor who came to observe the class, Carole Edelsky, also pointed out the ways in which Carl took up a power position in the class. For example, because Barbara wanted to be seen as facilitator and not as dispenser of information, she gave up the traditional seat at the head of the table to sit along the sides. Carole noticed that Carl occupied the seat at the head of the table, causing Barbara to realize that he took this seat at every session.

Further analysis of the audiorecordings also showed that Carl's conversational content, as well as his conversational style, showed gendered patterns. For example, at the beginning of each class, students often told stories of how they became aware of gender inequities inside and outside their own classrooms. Carl often dominated these discussions, casting himself as a hero. One such discussion focused on a female teacher in the school where he was teaching, and included a lengthy account of how he took over her class when she had a breakdown and settled her students and assumed her responsibilities. The content of Carl's talk reflected the common story line in gendered texts of women as victims and men as rescuers.

This experience caused Barbara to realize that simply reading and talking about gendered texts and talk was insufficient to change ingrained, gendered language behaviors. Although the primary purpose of the class was to raise participants' awareness of gendered texts and talk, there was still an underlying expectation that these students' heightened awareness would facilitate personal change. Barbara was reminded of a report of a study conducted by Donna Alvermann and her colleagues, including Josephine Young (who was then a doctoral student), in which they characterized disrupting gendered discourse as "easy to think about, difficult to do" (Alvermann, Commeyras, Young, Randall, & Hinson, 1997).

Like Barbara and Margaret, Josephine also examined males' gendered discourse. She (Young, 2000) conducted research for her doctoral dissertation by focusing on boys' reactions to texts that presented gendered and nongendered forms of masculinity. Josephine homeschooled her two young adolescent sons and two boys from next door for half the school year. During that time, she explored the boys' discourses about texts through activities that focused on masculinity. As the boys talked, they became more aware of the practice of masculinity and how masculine traits were portrayed in texts.

Josephine found that adolescent males' active displays of heterosexual, masculine practices hindered their participation in a critical analysis of stereotypical gender representations in texts. These boys were not always aware on their own of gendered identities and inequities in texts. Their conversations also revealed the influence of power relations among themselves, as well as within society, which contributed to their gendered preference for and interpretation of texts and their participation in literacy activity.

As a first year teacher, Laurie Fyfe (1999) also observed gendered behaviors in elementary school. Laurie observed a group of students in her fourth-grade classroom construct gender as they discussed a Chinese version of "Little Red Riding Hood." She noticed how children as young as 9 years old upheld gender stereotypes in how they interpreted the story. The children were unable to credit a female with having saved the day.

3

In an analysis of graduate students' literacy autobiographies, Marie Hardenbrook (1997) also discovered how gender influences reading. In another section of the Gender, Culture and Literacy class, Marie analyzed fellow students' reports of their experiences with electronic or computer text. Her analysis showed that reading and writing as a gendered practice was most prevalent in participants' reports of their experiences with electronic text. Women reported limited use of the computer (either used for e-mail access or not at all). Men, however, reported a much wider range of activities with electronic text, which included record keeping, Internet use (access to online catalogs), and use of CDs.

The investigations we (the authors of this book) undertook are described in more detail in the appropriate sections throughout this book. Despite our diverse experiences related to gender and literacy, our commonality was that each of us had been put in a position of learner through our roles as teachers or researchers. Our observations taught us how language and social contexts work to construct and reproduce gendered practice. What we had learned so far from our own observations surprised and interested us enough to come together to gain additional insights from the observations of others.

Others' Research

Given our experiences, we searched the literature to find how our observations compared to those of other researchers and teachers. We wanted to determine if our experiences were unique or typical of other U.S. classrooms. We were not surprised to find that there has been much national publicity about gender bias (asymmetrical opportunities for learning between the sexes) in classrooms.

We found that U.S. news reports like Dateline NBC's "Failing in Fairness" (1994) and national surveys of research by the American Association of University Women (e.g., American Institutes for Research, 1998; Haag, 1999) called attention to the ways in which students, particularly females, were often marginalized in instructional activity and talk about that activity. The American Association of Colleges (Hall & Sandler, 1982) presented results of a survey of a portion of the research on gender and education to publicize gender inequities in classrooms. Recent reports have drawn attention to how boys also were marginalized in classes such as language arts (e.g, Davies, 1997; Reed, 1999).

As a result, research on gender and literacy has become an agenda for researchers. Literacy researchers exploring literacy as a gendered social practice have found classroom discussion to be one of the most common ways in which those with less power are marginalized in instructional activity and talk about that activity (e.g., Alvermann, 1993; Alvermann & Commeyras, 1994; Orellana, 1995) (see Chapter 2). Researchers have investigated males' and females' discussions of texts and concepts in text in various content areas (e.g., literature and science), in a variety of settings (small group and whole class), in various grouping patterns (mixed-sex or same-sex), and with a variety of ages (e.g., high school and graduate students).

Literacy researchers also have examined the influence of gender on reading in a variety of ways. For example, several studies were conducted to determine males and females' reading preferences (e.g., Bardsley, 1999; Broughton, 1998; Brown, 1997; Christian-Smith, 1993) (see Chapter 3). These studies revealed students' gendered choices of trade books. Another area of inquiry has been the influence of gender on students' responses to fiction and nonfiction trade books, particularly in studies of literature response (e.g., Cherland, 1992, 1994; Davies, 1993; Nauman, 1997). Attempts to teach students to read against the text, or to read critically and challenge gender stereotypes, have been conducted with both groups of males (e.g., Young, 2000) and mixed-sex groups (e.g., Davies, 1989, 1993).

Researchers are also investigating the influence of gender on students' writing (see Chapter 4). The literature on gender and writing reveals that students' selection of topic, genre, and voice is usually divided by gender boundaries. As early as 1975, Donald Graves found differences in the free-choice writing topics of second-grade boys and girls. The girls in his study wrote frequently about themes and topics related to home, family, and friends. Boys wrote about themes and topics such as current events and sports. Graves's (1975) findings were repeated in other quantitative or experimental research throughout the 1980s (e.g., Many, 1989; Trepanier-Street & Ramatowski, 1999). Since then, qualitative or observational studies (e.g., Hunt, 1995; Kamler, 1994; MacGillivray & Martinez, 1998) have focused specifically on topic choice and gendered writing practices, such as voice and genre selection, which identify the same patterns in gendered writing as Graves found. More recent studies have focused on writing as a way to construct gendered identifiers and how gender influences writing evaluations (e.g., Cleary, 1996; Peterson, 1998).

A growing number of researchers are also exploring how gender influences students' readings of electronic texts, including their online discussions and writings (see Chapter 5). For example, Cynthia Lewis and Bettina Fabos (1999) explored middle school females' use of instant messaging. In addition, Marion Fey (1997, 1998) explored gender influences in her college students' online writings and discussions. In a feminist research project, Alice Christie (1995) attempted to change gendered patterns of students' writings by using online texts. Projects like these are practically significant because of documentation of greater electronic access taken, assumed by, or given to males (Gerver, 1984; Nielsen, 1994, 1998); teachers' steering of females to gender stereotypical uses of computer text, such as word processing (Nelson, 1990); and reports of sexual harassment with electronic text (Spender, 1995).

Another growing area of study focuses on the influence of gender on literacy development as revealed in literacy autobiographies (see Chapter 6). For example, literacy researchers reflected on their own gendered literacy development (Erickson et al., 1997), as have other researchers (Jackson, 1989/1990). Other investigators noted the influence of gender on literacy development by analyzing the literacy autobiographies of graduate students in literacy (e.g., Gritsavage, 1997; Guzzetti, 1997; Hardenbrook, 1997) or undergraduates in college composition (Sohn, 1998).

Our Purpose

Before now, the literature on gender and literacy had not been systematically analyzed or reviewed. We believed that a synthesis of these studies would be useful for several reasons. First, we thought that an analysis of findings within and across studies would raise awareness of gender issues in learning and practicing literacy, and add to our collective knowledge of the phenomena discovered in our own investigations. Second, we wanted to publicize successful interventions and recommendations for practice that would be useful for teachers and teacher

6

educators. Third, we wanted to find direction for our future inquiries, as well as provide direction to other researchers in gender and literacy by examining the unanswered questions of the existing research. Therefore, we undertook the task of systematically analyzing the literature on gender and literacy.

We confined our project to a review of the observational or qualitative research, particularly the feminist research, on gender and literacies by following procedures outlined for integrative reviews (see Jackson, 1980). Our review also became a critical review in that we systematically analyzed studies from a particular perspective or framework, identifying the silences in these studies, as well as the findings of these studies. Other critical reviews on different topics in literacy have been conducted by researchers such as Donna Alvermann (1986) and Marjorie Siegel (1989). Our review was intended to integrate the literature on gender literacies—discussion, reading, writing, electronic text, and literacy autobiography. In doing so, we anticipated being able to discover themes or patterns across studies that would lend new insights for the field.

Our Beliefs

We read various feminist theories and talked about them among ourselves until we could find a common theoretical ground on which to base our interpretation of the research. We conducted our review believing that gender pertains to the behaviors one performs to establish an association between one's sex and one's gender (Goffman, 1977). These behaviors (talking, dressing, body language) are embedded in all social interactions and informed by social contexts. Gender, then, refers to the accomplishment of managing the social activities individuals do to proclaim membership in a particular gender. Gender is something we do as we talk, act, read, and write in ways that constitute us as masculine or feminine within social structures (West & Zimmerman, 1987).

"Doing gender" produces and reproduces social differences between what is considered male and female. These differences are fairly stable along gender lines and become recognized as stereotypical or gendered. That does not mean, however, that there are any essential properties that exist outside of culturally and socially constructed categories of gender (Stanley & Wise, 1993). Instead, these differences begin to seem natural or essential because they are reproduced time and time again in our interactions with others and with texts (Butler, 1990). Like most feminists (Stanley & Wise, 1993), we do not distinguish between sex and gender because doing and reproducing gender happens from birth; therefore, we use the terms *gender* and *sex* interchangeably.

With these beliefs in mind, we analyzed the studies in this synthesis from the perspective of a feminist sociology, as explicated by Liz Stanley and Sue Wise (1993). This view of feminism was most consistent with our personal beliefs, was the most inclusive of the feminist theories we examined, and was compatible with the purpose of the review. This perspective within feminist sociology recognizes the researcher as interwoven with, changed by, and affecting the research; sees men and men's behaviors in their interactions with women as appropriate for study by feminists; presents a social-constructivist and nonessentialist view of gender; acknowledges multiple subjectivities; and purports that men, in their oppression of women, are themselves oppressed. For example, it was found that when males dominated instructional conversations they failed to learn a valuable educational tool—the skill of active listening (Guzzetti & Williams, 1996a, 1996b).

Our examples demonstrate how language and social contexts work to construct and reproduce gendered practices. As teachers, we believe that it is important to build students' awareness of how language constructs gender. We also believe that it is important to offer students opportunities to explore gendered identities in and through reading, writing, and discussion, and to deconstruct the categories of male and female. Although we find stereotypical categories of male and female limiting and work to deconstruct them, we believe, like Stanley and Wise (1993), that until women (and some men) are no longer oppressed, it is important to recognize categories of gender:

> [F]eminism should be concerned with the multiple and continual fractures that occur between experience and gender categories. This is partly because of the need to break hierarchical relationship of super- and subordination between them that when the two clash, it is experience which I [we] see as wrong. (p. 206)

In other words, we need categories so that we can compare them to our own experiences and uncover the possibilities of gender.

Limitations of Our Review

Our prior experiences as teachers, learners, and researchers shaped beliefs that influenced our interest in and conduct of this review. In some ways, those experiences facilitated our review. For example, our prior knowledge facilitated direction to pieces of the literature and to recommendations from individual researchers conducting these lines of inquiry. In other ways, however, our experiences limited our critical analysis because our beliefs led to a single framework. That framework is not all inclusive, nor does it necessarily match all the multiple frameworks we found in these studies. We do believe, however, that the filters we used to guide our data collection and analysis are compatible with the tenets of qualitative research in which the researcher, as the instrument, must describe bias, influence, and impact on the research, as well as offer "thick descriptions" (Erickson, 1988) of setting and context (Smith & Glass, 1987).

We limited our review in several other ways as well. First, we limited our project to a review of complete reports of qualitative or observational studies that investigated text or text-based activity with informants drawn from or situated in classrooms. We did so not because we believed some literacies to be more important than others, but to enable us to conduct an extensive yet manageable review. Therefore, this focus eliminated the small but growing number of studies of gender and other literacies (e.g., media literacy) but included more traditional literacies (e.g., reading and writing).

We realize that we were not able to include all the forms of research done on the topic of gender and the literacies that we focused on in our analysis. Because of limitations of space and time, we were unable to include studies that were content analyses from a gender standpoint of books or magazines, such as Kerry Carrington and Anna Bennett's (1996) revisionist analysis (examination of the positive and repressive effects) of popular magazines aimed at teenage girls in New Zealand and Australia. We also were not able to include the many theoretical or position papers, such as Pam Gilbert's (1992) analysis of gendered story writing and reading in Australia, or reflections on a particular researcher's own work, such as Alvermann and Anders's (1994) analysis of unexamined assumptions in content literacy from a feminist-critical perspective. We were also unable to include survey research.

9

In addition, several studies we wanted to include were unavailable. Most often, these were dissertations or articles from journals published outside the United States. Some, however, were simply unavailable in our libraries or computer searches.

Because of the vast body of research on gender and discussion, we also had to limit our review to those investigations that examined students' discussions of texts or concepts in texts. We chose only those studies of instructional discussion that examined interactions between students (and sometimes also between students and their teachers), and we analyzed those interactions by gender. We limited the review in this way because studies focusing exclusively on teacher-student interactions (e.g., Jungvarth, 1991; Sadker & Sadker, 1994) recommend changing only teachers' behaviors and did not address gender as a social construction that is formed and maintained by students in their interactions with each other.

Our Procedures

After deciding on a theoretical frame and limiting the scope of our study, our next step was to form an advisory council to assist us in refining the focus of the review, suggesting literature for the review, helping to develop a coding scheme for systematic analysis of the studies, and reading and reacting to our analysis. The advisory council consisted of researchers who are well known for research on gender and literacies: Donna Alvermann, University of Georgia; Patricia Anders, University of Arizona; and Carole Edelsky, Arizona State University.

Because these observational studies were often difficult to categorize, we developed guidelines for our classifications. Discussion studies were those studies that examined gender and language patterns (e.g., those conducted through some form of discourse analysis or sociolinguistic analysis). Reading studies were those studies that analyzed students' gendered reading practices and reactions to texts, as well as instructional methods that fostered these. Writing studies were those that focused on gender and the writing process, instruction in writing, or writing evaluation. Studies of electronic (posttypographical) text were classified as those that conducted a gender analysis of students' use of electronic communication. Literacy autobiographies

10

were confined only to those that analyzed gender as an influence on literacy development.

Given this focus, online and manual searches for published and unpublished studies were conducted in various databases, which included ERIC, UNCOVER, and Dissertation Abstracts International. In addition, hand searches of journals in education and literacy were conducted, including publications by the American Educational Research Association, International Reading Association, National Council of Teachers of English, and National Reading Conference. We also searched programs from professional conferences of the past 10 years. Other sources of studies included bibliographical branching and referrals from other researchers. Literature retrieval was conducted on the studies available through December 1999. Usually, each study was included only once in the analysis despite having appeared in more than one form (e.g., a dissertation that also appeared later as a published manuscript). In some cases, however, studies included more than one investigation or were so inclusive that portions could be coded in different categories (e.g., a study of both reading and discussion). In other cases, additional information or new analyses of the same data were reported in different reports. In these cases, the study was given two identification numbers, and components were coded separately.

During literature retrieval, we used sample studies to refine our coding scheme. We used our interests and our theoretical frameworks to identify each study's features to be coded. For example, because a feminist sociology presents a nonessentialist view of gender, we created items to examine age, ethnicity, social class, and gender of participants in each study. Because our view of feminist sociology holds that the researcher influences and is influenced by the research, we coded items pertaining to characteristics of the researcher, which included gender and ethnicity. We developed 36 codes amenable to quantitative analysis to provide descriptive statistics, including study demographics, such as setting (school, agency, home) and geographic location of study, as well as points of interest, such as type of qualitative study (ethnography, case study, teacher research); theoretical frame (poststructural feminist, social feminist, sociolinguistics); and form of report (journal article, dissertation, unpublished manuscript). In some cases, the theoretical frame was not stated directly, but was inferred based on the researchers cited or statements made by the author.

We relied on a structured procedure to classify the type of qualitative research represented in the study. We used established definitions by authorities to categorize a method. For example, we used Robert Stake's (1994) definition of *case study* as the complete study of an integrated and bounded system to classify a study as a case study, rather than simply using the author's claim. We used Frederick Erickson's (1985) definition of *ethnography* as the study of a complete life cycle of a culture or subculture to classify a study as ethnography. We used Susan Lytle and Marilyn Cochran-Smith's (1992) definition of *teacher research* to classify a study as teacher research. In cases in which studies did not fit one of these rubrics, we generically classified the study as qualitative research. In addition, some studies used a combination of qualitative and quantitative analyses; these were coded as combination.

After classifying and filing our studies, 13 studies were selected randomly from the research we gathered on gender and reading, writing, and discussion for interrater reliability. An analysis-of-discordance was conducted between five coders working on various aspects of the review. Particular items were discussed when disagreements were noted (usually in coding the type of qualitative research or inferring the theoretical frame). These procedures resulted in an eventual 92% to 96% intercoder agreement, dependent on type of study (reading, writing, or discussion).

An additional seven open-ended questions amenable to qualitative analysis were constructed for systematic coding. Three questions called for summaries, including study findings and researchers' assumptions and questions. Four questions were inferential, asking about the most surprising or insightful findings, connections to other research, critical analysis, and future directions for literacy education and research.

The items on the coding form assisted us in systematically analyzing the studies and organizing our review (see Appendix F). Results of our analysis from the codes most relevant to our review are reported in the study characteristics and themes sections of our report for each genre. (A table showing the results of the remaining codes is available from Barbara Guzzetti upon request.)

Because all project staff and advisory council members were European American women, we wished to expand our interpretation of the studies. Therefore, at least one study within the categories of reading, writing, and discussion was selected for coding by a literacy researcher of a different ethnicity or gender than our own. These external coders included Violet Harris, University of Illinois; David Moore, Arizona State University-West; Michael Smith, Rutgers University; and Beatrice Aires, Arizona State University. We asked a male researcher, for example, to code a study of females' small-group discussions. In some cases, we matched the ethnicity of the external coder to the ethnicity of the informants in the study. Intercoding ratings and comments were then compared and analyzed.

These external coders provided us with additional insights into the studies. For example, an external coder of a discussion study noted that the researchers identified no discrepant cases in their study of all-female discussion groups. In our own analysis, we remarked that no descriptions or comparisons were given for all-boy groups. Another external coder, a Hispanic female researcher, noted in her critique that a researcher conducting a study of Hispanic girls was unfamiliar with Latina feminism, thereby limiting the researcher's data collection and interpretation. Another external reviewer, a male researcher, interpreted a female student's writing differently than we did. When writing for her peers, the female used genderless references and self-censored topics that might offend a peer or make her appear too knowledgeable for a female. When writing for her teacher, however, she used gender referents and showed depth of knowledge. Our external male coder, however, interpreted this as an understanding of audience and a self-confident presentation. We interpreted that her writing for her peers indicated a lack of confidence and demonstrated that the power of social expectations limited her writing. In these ways, external coders' comments were helpful to us in our interpretations and critiques of the studies.

These codes and project staff members' codes were analyzed in several ways. First, a matrix (Miles & Huberman, 1984) was constructed that highlighted salient features, findings, and critiques of each study. This matrix was used to provide a general overview of the studies. In addition, codes for descriptive statistics of the studies (e.g., gender, age, and socioeconomic status of participants) were subjected to cross-tabs and frequencies analysis in SPSS (Statistical Package for the Social

Sciences). We analyzed the qualitative comments by reading and rereading these remarks and noting comparisons and contrasts between studies. We identified patterns across studies in ways similar to constant comparison (Glaser & Strauss, 1967). We found themes within and across studies of a particular genre (i.e., reading, writing, discussion). Notes were taken on these findings and discussed periodically among project staff. Our questions and remarks from these discussions were used to guide a rereading and reanalysis of the codes and comments.

Organization of Our Review

We present our findings and recommendations for each genre of studies (e.g., gender and discussion, gender and reading, gender and writing) separately because our readers may be more interested in findings from one type of study than another (see Chapters 2–6). For each genre of studies, we begin with the characteristics of the studies by providing descriptive statistics regarding each study's authors, samples, and methods. Next, we identify the themes found in our analysis of subsets of the studies and identify each of the studies that illustrates a particular theme. To be as succinct as possible, we describe only those studies that best represent the themes within each genre. In some cases, studies illustrated more than one theme; therefore, we describe the study under the theme it most illustrated. Following the identification of each theme and a description of the studies that illustrate these themes, we summarize and discuss these themes across the particular genre. Finally, we provide implications of these studies for research and instruction in the sections "Recommendations for Instruction" and "Recommendations for Research."

In Chapter 7, we summarize the studies across all genres. First, we characterize all the studies that we examined and call attention to the silences in those studies, as well as the findings. Second, we identify themes common across genres of studies (e.g., gendered discursive practices as a theme in studies of oral discussions is also identified as a theme in studies of electronic discussions). Finally, based on a cross-genre analysis, we offer recommendations for instructional practice and for the conduct and focus of future inquiries into gender and literacies.

CHAPTER 2

Studies on Gender and Discussion

Characteristics of the Studies

Since 1993, 30 qualitative studies were conducted that examined gender relations in students' discussions of texts. Most were conducted by female researchers. Of 45 authors, 80% of the first authors were female, 17% were male, and 3% were unknown. In 67% of the studies, at least one author's sex was not stated and had to be inferred by familiarity with the researcher/author. Similarly, in 76% of the studies, authors ethnicity was not stated. We were able to determine, however, that 47% of all authors were Caucasian, and 23% were African American. For the remaining 30% of researchers, ethnicity could not be determined. Only a few studies were done outside the United States, either in the United Kingdom (10%) or Canada (7%). Of these studies, 47% were published.

When researchers in the studies did not directly state their theoretical frameworks, frameworks were inferred from statements made and from authors cited by the researcher. Most of the studies were conducted from more than one theoretical frame, of which the most common were the theoretical frameworks of sociolinguistics or of language as a social practice (67% of the studies) or some form of feminism (67% of the studies). Of the feminist frames, poststructural feminism was the most common (40% of the feminist studies); the next most common frame was social constructivism (47%). Other frames included critical theory (7%), critical literacy (7%), and Piagetian constructivism (3%). In only five studies did authors describe themselves or their backgrounds and experience. Most of the research on gender and discussion was either qualitative (33%) or a combination of methods (20%). Investigators also conducted case studies (17%) or discourse analyses (17%). Of this research, 67% was published.

Most studies of gender and discussion were done with middle school or junior high students (36%) or done with elementary students (30%). High school students were 17% of the studies, whereas graduate students were 7%, and 10% focused on a combination of grade levels. Some studies investigated students in more than one subject, with 52% conducted in language arts and 28% in science. Studies in other content areas included social studies and geography (14%), mathematics (10%), content literacy (10%), and technology (3%). Sixty-seven percent of the studies included both males and females with 13% conducted with females only, and 3% with males only. Participants' sex in the other studies was not stated.

Only 27% of the studies of gender and discussion stated the participants' ethnicities, and 53% stated the participants' social class. Although many studies investigated informants representing several ethnicities and social classes, 62% included European Americans: 23% were from middle-class backgrounds, 17% upper-middle class, and only 13% were lower socioeconomic-status students. Researchers also studied African American (32% of the studies), Hispanic (6%), Asian (7%), Native American (3%), and biracial (3%) students.

Themes

Our analyses revealed five themes common among subsets of the observational studies on gender and discussion:

1. patterns of gendered discursive practice

2. gendered talk in literature-response groups

3. the stability of gendered discursive practice across content areas

4. the difficulties and dangers of interrupting gendered discursive practices

5. the problem of essentializing or assigning fixed or "natural" characteristics or behaviors to a particular gender

These themes are identified and exemplified in the following sections.

Patterns of Gendered Discursive Practice

Eight of these studies identified the language patterns by which females (and some males) were marginalized in classroom discussions (e.g., Alvermann, 1993, 1995; Evans, Alvermann, & Anders, 1998; Gritsavage, 1997a, also reported in 1997b; Guzzetti, 1996a, also reported in 1996b, 2001; Moore, 1997). For example, Barbara (Guzzetti, 2001) conducted observations and interviews of students and teachers in three high school physics classes: Physical World, a basic class for freshmen, and regular and honors physics for juniors and seniors. Although the teachers (one male and one female) had many years of teaching experience and had won district, state, or national awards for their teaching, they were unaware of any gender bias in their classrooms. Discussion patterns in the freshmen Physical World class, composed of approximately 50% Hispanic students and 50% European Americans, consisted of whole-class, recitation discussion. Boys asked questions of the teacher and occasionally of one another, whereas females usually put their heads down and went to sleep, waking only to do the seatwork. Discussion patterns in the junior and senior physics sections composed of primarily European Americans or foreign-born students were characterized by whole-class refutation discussions or small-group lab discussions of mixed-gender composition, both of which were dominated by the boys. In these sections, boys commonly interrupted girls, shouting out answers, disparaged girls' contributions, and gained and held the conversational floor. Girls tended to define participation as listening or recording the data, while boys set up and manipulated the equipment and made the observations. Only a few females spoke in whole-class discussions, although these tended to be the same girls each time. Donna Alvermann (1993, 1995) also reported this silencing of females in a study of students' peer-led discussions in language arts classes. In addition, Karen Evans and her colleagues (1998) found females silenced by males in small, mixed-sex groups during literature-response groups.

Margaret (Gritsavage, 1997a, 1997b) found similar patterns in her discourse analysis of seven adult participants' talk in her graduate course, Gender, Culture and Literacy. Four of these students were European American females ages 29, 32, 40, and 57. Two males were European Americans, ages 35 and 52; one 40-year-old male was African American. The researcher attempted to determine the conditions under which conversational dominance existed and how it was supported, constructed, and facilitated. To accomplish this, Margaret was a participant observer, audiorecording class members' talk about articles on gender and literacy that they had read for the course. She also audiorecorded the participants' talk at the beginning of each class about gender issues that touched their professional and personal lives. The researcher analyzed discourse episodes (units of discourse consisting of one or more connected topics) to determine language patterns.

Analysis of whose topics were initiated, whose talk held the floor, and whose topics were sustained showed that the oldest male in the class, Carl, dominated the talk. His share of the total conversation was about equal to that of the female professor's (30 compared to 35 new interjections). Carl was adept at steering the topic back to his issues and, for example, did so three times during a particular episode. To make his points, Carl interrupted the professor twice and a female student once. Carl was the only student who introduced topics unilaterally rather than collaboratively.

This study showed that simply reading and talking about gender issues in discussion did not change participants' established patterns of gendered discussion, which supported a singly developed, floor-facilitated, hierarchal interaction and reproduction of dominance and subordination. In addition, discourse patterns appeared to be influenced by participants' ages as well as genders.

Another study, conducted by David Moore (1997), described how high school students both accepted and contested gendered interactions. Moore observed a 12th-grade, advanced-placement, senior English class that consisted of nine females and four males of mixed ethnicities. His report focused on two students, a male (Alex), and a female (Heather), who were prominent contributors and well regarded by classmates and the teacher. He analyzed literacy events using a guide constructed of categories formed from his data. These categories included social and intellectual relationships, conversational moves, and conversational contents to assist in identifying language patterns in discussions.

Moore found that Alex and Heather exemplified language patterns typically associated with males and females. For example, Heather contested traditional notions of gender-appropriate behavior by breaking away from gender-typical language, taking the conversational floor, and holding it for some time. She dominated the classroom, and exerted her will by reading a story that was not related to the day's curricular topic and by initiating the story without the teacher's permission. She acted as the reporter for her small group when they shared their outcomes, and she forcefully voiced her opinions during class discussions. Heather also, however, demonstrated gender-typical actions by indicating a self-in-relation-to-others subjectivity by showing others a story that she liked to validate her opinion. She referred to the story using the word *cute*, which is a stereotypical adjective, and deprecated the passage with the qualifier, "It just says" (p. 520). Heather valued discussions because they provided connections she could make with what she read.

Alex also displayed language typical of both males and females. For example, he had a tendency to produce the final word about the meaning of things and to interrupt others to build collaboratively on their train of thoughts—language behaviors typically associated with males. He exhibited rapport, which is said to be characteristic of females, as well as report, which is said to be characteristic of males. Alex encouraged Heather to read a story she wanted to read, which could be interpreted as giving access to the conversational floor and sharing or granting conversational rights, an authoritative transfer of power. In doing so, he exercised power by sharing it. Alex valued discussions because they helped him distinguish between correct and incorrect thinking about main points in passages.

Moore concluded by recommending that teachers address the social relationships that students bring with them when interacting with print. Teachers should help students to identify and reflect on possible gendered practices in language. Educators can call attention to face-to-face interactions related to literacy by modeling how to encourage contributions to a discussion and build on others' statements.

Gendered Talk in Literature-Response Groups: Group Composition Issues

Seven studies addressed gender issues related to peer-led literature circles or literature-response groups (see Alvermann, Young, &

Green, 1997; Cherland, 1992; Evans, 1999; Marks, 1995; O'Donnell & Smagorinsky, 1999; Phelps & Weaver, 1999; Smith, 1998). In these studies, the practice of literature response was interpreted as peer-led groups, particularly those in which students aimed to relate to the characters by drawing from their own experiences. For example, Meredith Cherland (1992) observed literature-response groups in sixth-grade classes in a Canadian middle-class area to examine males' and females' patterns of discourse during their talk about fiction at school. Cherland audiorecorded and transcribed literature-response groups and analyzed the content and the quantity of the talk by a content analysis, and by calculating a mean length of turn for each participant.

Cherland found that these children enacted their understandings of gender during their talk in literature-response groups. For example, in every mixed-gender group, the person with the highest average length of turn was a boy, even when there was only one boy in the group. All girls averaged shorter turns in mixed-gender groups than in all-girl groups. Boys in the mixed-gender groups attained averages that were higher than the highest average demonstrated by a girl in these same mixed-gender groups. Conversely, all the girls had averages lower than the lowest boy's average. All girls took their greatest number of turns in the all-girl group.

Cross-gender teasing also was used in the groups to mark and maintain gender boundaries. Teasing consisted of speaking in a group in a way that intentionally provoked or irritated another person about something not significant to the group as a whole. Only two cases of teasing occurred in nine of the same gender groups. On the other hand, 13 instances of teasing took place in 5 of the mixed-gender groups, and only 1 case of teasing occurred in an all-boys group. In the all-girls group, teasing occurred only once. Instances of teasing included a boy (Michael) teasing girls (Julie and Lisa) for missing details in the text and for giggling about reindeer when they were mentioned in the story. When these girls expressed disgust at the fact that the characters in the novel they were reading were forced to eat raw rabbit meat to prevent starvation, Aaron and Michael teased them about eating sushi. Cherland concluded that the fact that more teasing occurred in the mixed-gender groups was significant because it appeared that deference or dominance was more relevant when both genders were present in a group. The fact that teasing almost always involved both sexes possibly indicated that teasing was being used as a strategy for establishing dominance, demonstrating the power to provoke, annoy, belittle, scorn, or laugh at another.

Similar patterns were noted with contradictions, or any statement that disagreed with and went against the meaning of the previous speaker's statement. As with teasing, much more contradiction occurred in mixed-gender groups than in same-gender groups, and almost all instances of contradiction occurred in cross-gender interactions. There were no contradictions in all-boy groups and few in the all-girls' groups. Like teasing, contradictions most often placed the sexes in opposition to each other, creating antagonism between the gender groups.

In another study, Karen Evans, Donna Alvermann, and Patricia Anders (1998) addressed teasing in literature-response groups. These researchers described the experience of three fifth-grade girls during their classroom literature discussions to illustrate how gender influences students' interpretations of texts, and how issues of voice and empowerment can become problematic within the context of peer-led literature-discussion groups. Students selected a book to discuss, kept literature-response logs, and used these logs to facilitate their discussions. Because several groups met at the same time, the teacher rotated among groups rather than spending extended time with any one group.

Two girls, Mimi and Vivianne, were members of the same discussion group that also included three boys. During the first days of discussion, Vivianne appeared to assume a leadership role, often refocusing comments and using direct overtures to get the group back on task when discussion was wandering off task. At first, Mimi also actively participated by initiating most topics and by having her contributions responded to by others. On the third day of discussion, however, when a change in topic occurred, it dramatically changed the dynamics of the group. The boys in the group teased Mimi, which she tried to stop with strategies such as physical response, verbal retaliations, and threats to tell the teacher. Both Mimi and Vivianne tried to refocus the group back to the book, but their attempts and methods were unsuccessful. On the fourth day, one boy challenged Vivianne's attempts to keep the group on task; consequently, Vivianne chose silence as a means of self-protection.

Evans and her colleagues (1998) noted that the boys' attempts to silence voices were only directed at the girls in the group and never at each other. The girls formed an alliance in their efforts to protect each other from the boys' teasing and marginalizing tactics. For example, when Mimi was the target of the boys' teasing, Vivianne used refocus comments to move the conversation back to the book. When the boys challenged Vivianne, Mimi rose to her defense, by telling the boys to "shut up." The girls also sat together, facing the three boys who sat on the other side of the circle. The researchers concluded that reader-response strategies, such as literature-discussion groups, "often reinforce sexist stereotypes that the discussions are designed to interrupt" (p. 117). This study added to the literature that suggests that high school and middle school girls usually play a submissive role in literature-discussion groups.

Stephen Phelps and Dera Weaver (1999) also investigated peer-led literature-discussion groups. The purpose of their study of two discussion formats (teacher-directed, mostly whole-class discussions and recitations in history, and peer-led small-group discussions of literature) was to examine the influences on the degree to which students' personal voices became public talk in classrooms. Phelps, Weaver, and teachers in an eighth-grade classrooms conducted teacher research by observing peer-led literature discussions. The researchers focused on two females (Laura and Alice) and one male (Brad), three of the most talkative students, as they and their classmates discussed plot elements in Robert Louis Stevenson's *Dr. Jekyll and Mr. Hyde* in a teacher-assigned and peer-led literature-discussion group. Vignettes written by these students illustrated cases in which students seemed unable or unwilling to participate in the public discourse of the classroom, as well as focused students' views on what motivates students to either participate or not in class discussions.

The vignette most relevant to this review described how Laura became marginalized as a speaker in her attempt to tell a story because Brad kept interrupting her with corrections of her details. Laura, who felt challenged by Brad's insistence on his own description of the book, was drawn into an argument with Brad about the significance of the door to the house where Mr. Hyde enters the laboratory of Dr. Jekyll. Brad characterized Laura's attempts to voice her opinion as being "whiney." Even other females complained about how much Laura talked, her tendency to talk over the group, and her proclivity to argue a point. Other students made fun of Laura, and because Laura realized this, it resulted in her lack of desire to speak and her loss of voice.

The teacher researchers (Phelps & Weaver, 1999) reflected on Laura's dilemma and on the tension between allowing freedom of speech and maintaining control:

> I used to feel sad about what happened to Laura in those discussions. I feared that my interest in peer-led discussions placed her in harm's way by removing from this lively, opinionated, and verbal class the kinds of restraints that a teacher can so easily place on classroom discussion. I worried that I had abdicated my responsibility to make the classroom a safe place for every child.... If I had been alone, without a team of fellow researchers available for encouragement and support, I might have stepped back from peer-led discussion after this incident. Although I now see my act of placing Laura, Brad and Alice together "just to see what would happen" as irresponsible and arrogant on my part, I also know that my wish to protect and shelter is, in every area of classroom life but physical safety, just as self-centered and wrong. As teachers, we are responsible for initiating students into the ethics of talk. The issues that constitute democratic political culture are only seized and debated by those who feel they have something to say, those who feel confident in their ability to listen, analyze and understand. Our students will never find their own balance of public and personal voice if they are not given frequent opportunities to explore a variety of roles and positions, even if some of the explorations take them into dangerous territory. (p. 352)

The researchers concluded that there are risks associated with encouraging personal voices. Although a teacher may be aware of these risks and try to minimize them, the risks of joining in public discourse cannot be eliminated altogether. Learning cannot be made entirely safe for all students.

In a year-long study, Karen Evans (1999) investigated peer-led literature-discussion groups in a fifth-grade classroom of 11 girls and 11 boys, 73% of whom were European Americans from working-class neighborhoods. Evans cotaught lessons with the teacher, observed and videotaped literature-discussion groups, and met with groups to watch and comment on segments of their discussions from the preceding day. Evans asked questions to determine if and how other members of the group influenced individuals' participation in literature-discussion groups.

Evans reported three findings. First, students had a clear notion of the conditions that are conducive to effective discussions. Students cited needing basic requirements, like reading the book and writing in their literature journals in order to have something to report in discussion. Students also mentioned respect issues, like listening to each other and not interrupting. In addition, individuals preferred to work with people they could work with, particularly friends with whom they could feel comfortable voicing their opinions. Reading a book they liked also helped. Second, students noted that the gender composition of discussion groups influenced how they participated in and experienced their literature discussions. A mixed-gender group often hindered students' ability to engage in productive discussions; that is, girls consistently withdrew from discussions, reporting that boys' attitudes were the problem. One girl reported,

> David has to have everything perfect, everyone has to read to just the right spot and have their journal and participate and if it's not perfect, you can't do anything. And Sean always takes David's side. We had read most of the [assignment], but David got mad because we hadn't read the whole thing. (1999, p. 12)

In all the mixed-gender groups that struggled, the girls sat on one side and the boys on the other, often refusing to look at each other. Videotapes showed the students directing glares and disgusted looks toward the other sex. In several groups, males and females actually split off from each other and removed themselves to form two smaller same-gender groups. Both girls and boys reported preferring same-gender groups. Those who were members of both types of groups during the year consistently reported being better able to enact the conditions for a successful group in same-gender groups. These students felt more comfortable around members of the same sex. Girls reported feeling shy and embarrassed around boys they liked. Girls also expressed fears that boys would laugh at and make fun of their opinions. Both boys and girls preferred same-gender groups because they perceived that boys and girls have different ideas and talk about different topics. For example, one girl reported that boys elaborated on a subject like sports; a boy commented that girls have different opinions than boys do. Girls expressed this same concern in a story about domestic violence, fearing that boys might have thought the violence was cool and ruin the discussion for the girls.

In accordance with these reports, Evans found that 5 of the 7 most effective groups were same-gender groups, and 7 of the 10 struggling groups were mixed-gender groups that had split along gender lines. Gender issues were usually the main reasons for difficulties in a discussion group. Girls reported that some of their own behaviors (such as not reading) inhibited their peer-led groups' discussions.

Evans's final finding was that bossy group members had negative influences on literature-discussion groups. Bossy members could be either male or female. Bossy members were those who told others what to do, did not give others a chance to read from their journals, and prohibited the group from hearing what others had to say. Bossy group members were problematic only in mixed-gender groups; students never mentioned this problem in same-gender groups. Students who were bossy in mixed-gender groups were not bossy in same-gender groups. The students distinguished between bossy members and leaders. Leaders facilitated and organized the group, whereas bossy people talked too much. Those who were members of the most effective groups were less likely to need a leader, preferring that everyone share leadership responsibilities.

Evans reflected on how the research affected her as a teacher and a researcher. She questioned what students learned from their experiences in peer-led literature-discussion groups when conflict between genders escalated and went unresolved. Evans wondered what students learned from emphatically expressing their desires to be in same-gender groups, yet still finding themselves placed in mixed-gender groups. Evans reported feeling uncomfortable with what students likely learned about issues of power, gender, and teacher authority, wondering if some of these experiences were "mis-educative" for students. Although Evans stated that she did not advocate discontinuing the practice of peer-led literature-discussion groups, she acknowledged the need to re-examine how gender issues affect students' experiences in instruction. Evans suggested that future studies investigate holistically the social context of literature-discussion groups. Teachers should ask themselves how conditions such as gendered language and bossy students can be attended to when forming discussion groups, and explore ways to provide for all students to have equal opportunities for participation. As a teacher of preservice teachers, Evans found impetus from her study to inform her students that by listening to and observing their own students, they can learn much about how to teach.

Three other studies advocated discussions through reader response, but in same-sex groups (Marks, 1995; O'Donnell-Allen & Smagorinsky, 1999; Smith, 1998). For example, Cindy O'Donnell-Allen and Peter Smagorinsky (1999) examined reader-response groups composed of four females (two white, one African American, and one Native American) in a senior English class to examine how these girls established ways of working together that enabled them to discuss and interpret the character Ophelia in Shakespeare's *Hamlet*.

Initially, the girls' language was characterized as tentative, nurturing, connected, and indirect; for example, they offered their story-analysis plans as possibilities rather than directives. Girls acknowledged and built on each other's contributions and responded to each other's self-deprecating comments with reassurances. Over time, their language patterns changed from tentative and suggestive to analytical and directive. These females demonstrated a synthesis of ideas through dialectic discussion, constructing knowledge and collaborating through supportive and inclusive speech. The researchers concluded by advocating small-group settings, open-ended tasks such as dialogue journals and student-led discussions for girls in same-gender groups.

In another study, Sally Smith (1998) conducted a reader-response group to examine how early adolescent girls respond to books through talk in a book club. Smith's informants were sixth-grade girls. The group expanded over time from four to nine girls. Two participants were African American, one was biracial, one Hispanic, and one Hispanic/European American; others were European American. The researcher selected books that were a combination of the canon (classics) and children's and young adult novels, which included oppositional views to the traditional and unquestioned portrayals of marginalized groups, such as females. Smith conducted one-on-one interviews four times with each girl, and audiorecorded their weekly discussions. She replayed segments of taped discussions and asked girls to respond to and analyze their conversations and taped interviews.

Readings and intimate discussions in a small group prompted storytelling (matching personal or read experiences to text themes) and testifying (explication of values and beliefs). Storytelling of personal experiences and perspectives, particularly rejection of racial stereotypes, enabled these girls to speak openly and freely in reader response. Participants and their language arts teachers reported increased participation of the book club members in their classes.

In a combination qualitative and quantitative study, Tracey Marks (1995) also investigated gender differences in six third-graders' peer-led, mixed- and same-gender literature-discussion groups. The researcher facilitated literature-discussion groups by following a conversational discussion-group approach (O'Flahavan, 1989). Discussions had three phases: introduction and review, discussion, and debriefing about the discussion itself. Marks videotaped peer-led literature-discussion groups, interviewed students, asked them to respond to the videos, and drew sociograms to understand students' performance and perceptions of gender differences in discussion of texts.

Marks found that boys spoke more than girls did in mixed-gender groups. Unlike the girls, boys used language that monitored their group interactions more in the same-gender group than in mixed-gender groups. In mixed-gender groups, girls assumed the roles of elicitors, which encouraged others to participate in the discussions. Boys discussed certain topics of personal experience and used particular kinds of discourse, like tag questions (traditionally associated with females) more frequently than did girls. Girls viewed the boys as group leaders and preferred to participate in same-gender discussions. Marks recommended that teachers increase students' awareness of gender issues by raising and discussing these issues, and broaden their teaching strategies to include those that make females feel comfortable assuming both masculine and feminine stances.

Donna Alvermann, Josephine Young, and Colin Green (1997) conducted Read and Talk Clubs to study discursive practices of adults and adolescents in out-of-school discussions of texts. The researchers found that which gender spoke most depended on the type of text being discussed. Females excluded males from discussions about texts written for females, such as the Sweet Valley High series. Contrary to typical patterns in which males silence females, girls silenced boys in the group by not acknowledging the boys' comments as informative or credible. Hence, the type of text under discussion may influence the patterns of discussion in informal settings.

The Stability of Gendered Discursive Practice Across Content Areas

Eight studies examined patterns of gendered interactions in content areas other than reading or language arts (Guzzetti & Williams, 1996a, 1996b, 2001; Holden, 1993; Meyer & Fowler, 1993; Tolmie & Howe, 1993; Wilkinson, Lindow, & Chang, 1985; Wilson & Haug, 1995). These studies attempted to address the stability of gendered discursive practices across content areas, and found on the whole that patterns of gendered discussion are similar across content areas. For example, Andrew Tolmie and Christine Howe (1993) observed the dialogue of 12- to 15-year-old students in the United Kingdom while they worked in pairs using computer texts about the paths of falling objects. Dyads were composed of 13 male pairs, 12 female pairs, and 16 mixed-sex pairs. Their dialogues were videotaped and analyzed qualitatively and quantitatively to determine if there were any differences by gender in opinion exchanges, and, if so, whether those differences affected academic performance.

The researchers found that males learned most when initial differences over predictions led to exchange of views, whereas female pairs did not resolve conflicting predictions, and used avoidance strategies to ignore discrepancies in their explanations. Females avoided conflict, while males asserted and elaborated when faced with conflict. Mixed-gender pairs also avoided conflict and did better the less they said. Constraints on their interactions increased with their ages. These researchers recommended structuring discussions with specific prompts at strategic points.

Another British researcher, Cathie Holden (1993), examined patterns of talk by gender in small groups in mathematics and technology, as well as language arts, to determine differences in boys' and girls' talk in small groups. Thirty audiorecordings were made of 4- to 11-year olds' discussions. Transcripts were analyzed using a category system, which classified talk as action talk, noncollaborative talk (talking to oneself), and collaboration in abstract (using abstract language to reason, hypothesize, and conclude).

Holden found that both boys and girls verbally contributed differently, depending on the curriculum, but language patterns were gendered. For example, boys spoke less often in language arts classes than did girls, but more than girls in mathematics and technology classes. Girls' abstract talk was depressed in each curriculum area when the group contained more boys than girls.

In a similar study, Louise Wilkinson, Janet Lindow, and Chi Pang-Chang (1985) examined gender differences in peer-led discussion groups in mathematics. They looked at ways in which language was used to request and receive information and action, and to engage in verbal disagreements. To do so, the researchers analyzed 20 videotapes of six mixed-sex groups' discussions and focused particularly on dissension episodes or interactions following a verbal disagreement about an answer to a problem during small-group work. Informants were second- and third-grade students, grouped by gender and ability, in a middle-class predominantly white neighborhood in the midwestern United States. Quantitative analyses were conducted to determine differences between boys and girls' same-sex and cross-sex interactions, and qualitative analyses were done to determine interpretations of the quantitative findings

Boys' answers prevailed more often in dissension episodes than did girls' answers. Boys made many more requests for action and information to boys than to girls. They received, however, neither more nor fewer appropriate responses from either sex. Girls made equal numbers of requests of boys and girls. The researchers determined that boys' answers prevailed most often because they were correct. There was also evidence of boys insulting girls' answers. The researchers believed that some episodes of disagreement (such as one characterized by giggling, touching, and joking) served a primarily social function. The researchers concluded that boys' preferences for same-sex interactions might result in patterns of sex segregation. These researchers advocated teaching students to be aware of their communication processes through simulated recalls.

In a study with similar findings, John Wilson and Brian Haug (1995) analyzed the talk of middle school students, who were placed in four pairs by gender and ability (high or low). Dyads were given texts from science, English, and geography, asked to read them, and then re-present them in another form, such as illustrations, tables, charts, or drawings. Students audiorecorded their own conversations that were categorized by the researchers as reciprocal, argumentative, hypothetical, referential, or interpretative.

The most striking contrast between the sexes was in the argumentative mode. Both ability groups among the boys generated high proportions of argumentative talk. Both girls' groups barely showed any willingness or need to argue. Low-ability girls spent the greatest proportion of the their time between the hypothetical and interpretative modes, in contrast to the rest of the groups who spent 12% or less time in these modes. Girls exhibited more referential talk than did boys, by referring to the text directly or reading from the passage. Low-ability girls also had the lowest scores for reciprocal talk or talk that recognizes others' views, which contradicted the idea that females talk collaboratively. The researchers recommended that students be taught to examine their talk and why they prefer different modes.

Debra Meyer and Paula Fowler (1993) conducted a study to determine the extent to which language differences and similarities among boys and girls were associated with their sex, the content area being discussed, and the teacher's responses to students. They observed and audiorecorded sixth graders in teacher-led whole-class discussions in mathematics and social studies. They conducted a linguistic analysis to examine associations between linguistic category (coded for purpose as declarative, interrogative, imperative, or exclamatory and form as simple, compound, complex, and compound-complex) by content area and gender. In addition, Meyer and Fowler extensively examined the talk of two students (one girl and one boy) who participated most frequently in both the math and social studies classes.

Differences were found between sexes and content areas. Both boys and girls demonstrated fewer elaborations or extensions in math than in social studies. Girls asked more questions involving elaborations in social studies than did boys. Boys participated more in math when the talk was about procedures. The female student, who Meyer and Fowler studied extensively, demonstrated an ability to change her discourse style to match the content. In math, she did so with indicative comments by voicing her ideas and questioning why she had missed problems—typically male moves appropriate to mathematics. The male student, however, showed discourse of a procedural or performance nature in math, neither of which were productive in facilitating knowledge growth.

The Difficulties and Dangers of Interrupting Gendered Discursive Practices

Nine studies conducted by five university researchers and four teacher researchers attempted to change the patterns or content of gendered discussions of texts. These studies were conducted primarily with European American, middle-class students, including primary elementary, upper elementary, middle school, high school, and graduate students. Interventions were attempted in language arts and literature discussions (Alvermann, 1995; Alvermann, Commeyras, Young, Randall, & Hinson, 1997; Evans et al., 1998), a home-schooling project (Young, 2000), elementary science (Gallas, 1995), and high school science classes (Guzzetti, 2001; Guzzetti & Williams, 1996a, 1996b), and a graduate course in content literacy (Alvermann, Young, et al., 1997).

All the researchers alluded to or spoke directly to the dangers of intervening in gendered discursive practices. A common finding across these studies was that power relations among students influenced students' discourse. Those with the most power got the floor more often, held the floor longer and more often, and determined who voiced an opinion, how it was voiced, whose comments were elaborated on, and whose remarks were dismissed. Consequently, these researchers attempted to change these patterns of gendered discussion. Inevitably, their interventions became attempts to change power relations among students. The following findings illustrate why Alvermann, Young, and their colleagues characterized these attempts as "easy to think about, difficult to do" (p. 73).

One recommendation in the literature on gender and discussion has been to use small groups for classroom discussion to give females greater voice in classroom activity and talk about that activity (e.g., Nelson, 1990; Tannen, 1995). After documenting asymmetrical participation in whole-class discussions of classes composed mostly of European American middle-class students, a male, European American, high school physics teacher researcher, and a university researcher (Guzzetti & Williams, 1996a, 1996b, 2001) compared females' participation in small groups to their participation in whole-class discussions. These researchers found that when only one male was present, females merely recorded the data, whereas males read the computer texts, set up the equipment, and made the observations. When students were grouped by gender, however, females talked collaboratively and symmetrically among each other. This increased tendency to talk did not carry over to whole-class discussions, however, in which females resumed their patterns of silence, defining their participation as listening.

Why were these researchers unable to affect a transfer of this increased self-confidence that females displayed together (as they reported in interviews) to whole-class discussions in which males were present? Students answered that question by their comments and behaviors that addressed the risks and losses associated with interrupting gendered discursive practices. Individual girls who complained to the female researcher on a one-to-one basis refused to discuss as a class (in a mixed-gender group) the ways in which boys marginalized them (e.g., females who challenged the opinions of males were considered by those males as "whiney"). Females spoke of the risk of damaging their reputations that would result from such confrontation. Males appeared proud of their oppression of the female students. For example, when shown comments from females such as, "The boys are loud and immature" (Guzzetti & Williams, 1996b, p.15), a group of males in one section of physics broke out in unified song. They sang a toy store ad song that had words to the effect, "I don't want to grow up, I don't want to grow up, 'cuz if I did, I couldn't be a Toys 'R' Us kid." When asked why they did that, one of the male singers and one female student stated that it was to celebrate male bonding and male superiority in the class.

Therefore, to acquiesce to females would imply a loss of male privilege. Young men in the class seemed to recognize this, and made comments on their questionnaires such as, "Boys rule the class." Despite teachers' attempts to be gender fair, the culture of the classroom can subvert or override those attempts. Efforts to change these gendered patterns may actually serve to reinforce those practices. Guzzetti and Williams (1996b) concluded by recommending that discussion occur in small groups by gender and that students be involved in creating solutions to gender bias in discussion.

In another report, Josephine (Young, 2000) documented evidence of students' and a teacher's reluctance to address gender bias in instructional discussion. In a home-schooling project in which she used critical literacy activities to challenge middle school boys' stereotypical notions of gender, Josephine found that her informants were disinterested in and uncomfortable talking about gender. One male reported that his discomfort arose from not being able to find the words to describe his reactions. Another male reported that such dialogues were uncomfortable because he had not thought about these issues before. Judy Norris-Handy (1996) reported similar findings for boys in a social studies class who struggled with their public personas versus their private voices in mixed-gender groups.

Power relations among Josephine's small group of adolescent males also influenced the number and content of the boys' remarks about gender. For example, one boy changed his opinion about the acceptability of boys crying, afraid to match the gendered value statements made by his friend in the group. Critical literacy activities were successful in transforming the boys' awareness of gendered identities and inequities only when masculine practices portrayed in texts did not match their own experiences. When masculine practices in texts matched their own practices, discussion of these experiences simply reinforced and confirmed those practices. The boys' reluctance to disturb their own notions and actions of gender was representative of their reluctance to talk about gender issues.

Another teacher researcher, Daryl Morrison (1995), used literature that exposed oppression and marginalization, and conducted critical literacy activities to challenge sexist, racist, and classist attitudes, language, and behaviors. He studied the reactions of 28 white third-grade students in a rural environment to literature that dealt explicitly with social issues, such as gender, race, and class. Morrison defined critical literacy using Henry Giroux's (1995) description of activity that involves the skills of deconstructing texts, how they signify and produce meaning, and how they influence and shape their readers. To meet this goal, Morrison selected four pieces of literature that used gender, race, and class to illuminate unequal relations of power. These books included stories such as *Piggybook* (Browne, 1986) in which the father and two boys act like pigs, which caused their mother to leave until the males in the household decide to help with housework. Morrison read these books to the students, and they discussed them. The students also recorded their questions in a diary.

Initial discussions were dominated by question-answer dialogue. Morrison was disappointed. No students questioned their own situations in regard to class or race. Some students expressed their resistance to challenge a text by asking questions (who, what, when, where) that exemplified typical patterns of traditional literature. Overall, however, exposure to literature that touched on oppression, marginalization, dominance, and silence empowered students to challenge one another, as well as the literature and its authority. Students monitored one another's opportunities to speak in class discussions of text, and they engaged in true discussions (i.e., students talked with each other, and responded in phrases and sentences rather than monosyllables).

Donna Alvermann, Michelle Commeyras, Josephine Young, Sally Randall, and David Hinson (1997) described another intervention. The researchers reported one of two investigations in the same study in which participants did not want to address gender issues in discussions of texts. Gender issues were not "a burning issue" (p. 100) for either the female teacher or the students in a middle school language arts class. The teacher stated that she was ill-prepared to discuss gender issues and found resulting discussions to be awkward and contrived. She also reported feeling uncomfortable challenging the community's dominant cultural values of family and preferred a neutral stance.

The male teacher in the study also preferred a neutral stance. In his middle school language arts class, required readings of mixed-race, class, and gender issues drew passionate remarks. A few students, however, reported such talk as unrelated to their purpose for enrolling in the course. The majority of the class showed their discomfort with subsequent discussions of this nature by being more reserved in their comments. Students excluded each other's ideas during discussions that were intended to challenge students' stereotypical patterns of heterosexist thinking (e.g., what constitutes masculinity). The teacher's attempts to interrupt gendered discursive practices actually seemed to further embed those gendered discursive behaviors in their discussions. For example, one boy stated, "Since we've been talking about sexism, the girls got their own point of view and boys got their own, and we're always against each other" (Alvermann, Commeyras, et al., 1997, p. 97).

Attempts to provide more symmetrical opportunities for students' participation in class discussion in a content literacy class (Alvermann, Commeyras, et al., 1997) resulted in a dilemma when attempting to treat all students equally. One intervention these researchers attempted was to allocate the same amount of time for each speaker presenting a project report. A foreign-born female found that due to her language difficulty, she was unable to express her ideas in the same amount of time as those in the class who were native speakers. Therefore, attempts like these to treat everyone the same and be equal can result in inequities among students, an insight also reported by Deborah Tannen (1990).

Another teacher researcher, Karen Gallas (1995), attempted to intervene in asymmetrical discussions in elementary science classes. She reported some success with using metacommunication (discussing with her students the marginalizing aspects of audiorecorded classroom discussions) and techniques (e.g., wait time, rephrasing answers) to self-monitor students' own participation in discussions. She described one boy who in the process of abdicating some of his power, as evidenced by strong assertions, was able to give voice to creative and imaginative, although tentative, ideas. Gallas raised the question of to what extent rearranging power relations is liberating for those who are essentially powerless and voiceless. Although she reported that formerly reticent girls experimented with more public kinds of talk, our analysis of the transcripts of data provided by Gallas showed that females' ideas were referenced or elaborated on only by other females.

Alvermann (1993) also questioned the notion that power is a commodity that can be transferred or imposed on others by an authority like a teacher. She reported on a teacher's efforts to give an articulate student with a tendency to talk more opportunities to do so. As time passed, this boy talked less and less, perhaps because other students silenced or showed their displeasure at his attempts to contribute to group discussions. He blamed his teacher for enfranchising him as a speaker. Alvermann cautioned that prompting students to voice their ideas might not be as empowering as teachers might think.

Evans's 1998 study illustrated Gore's (1993) notion that although power cannot be bestowed, power can be used to help others exercise power. Girls in an all-female literature-discussion group tried to include a silent female in their discussion. They attempted to give her voice by asking her direct questions and asking her to share her ideas, encouraging her as a valued member of their group. When she failed to respond, these females did not exercise their power to dominate or devalue her. Rather, they accepted her view of participation as listening. Silence was used by this female as a legitimate participation style, which allowed her to be comfortable when uncomfortable speaking. Females used silence as a way of helping each other and allowing females to exercise their power.

Conversely, in a mixed-gender group, boys were not exercising their power to help the girls, but to stop the girls from exercising their power by teasing and challenging them. Hence, these researchers concluded that the nature of literature discussions often reinforces sexist stereotypes. Ironically, it is these kinds of gendered stereotypes that the discussions are designed to interrupt.

Challenges to Essentialist Notions of Gender and Discussion

Overwhelmingly, in the literature for the lay public, we are bombarded with notions that males are essentially different than females, and that females behave and talk in one way and males in another (Gray, 1997; Tannen, 1986, 1990). The notion is that if we could just understand males' and females' conversational styles, then misunderstandings in classrooms, workplaces, and marriages would be eliminated and communication would be improved. These ideas of inherent gender characteristics are referred to as essentialism, reflecting a belief in the existence of fixed and essential properties for each gender that are constructed either biologically or naturally by human nature (Stanley & Wise, 1993). Researchers engage in essentialism when they do not describe the multiple subjectivities of their informants, particularly informants' ethnicity, race, or class, yet present their findings in ways that infer logical generalizability. Most researchers in gender and discussion studied European Americans (60% of the studies in this category), but did not qualify their findings as limited to this group. As noted previously, 25% of the authors of gender and discussion studies did not specify the ethnicity of their informants, which implied that this information was not important, or that findings were characteristic of students of all types within the age group studied.

Four of the 30 studies were exceptions and spoke to issues of gender and discussion with African American students (Hinchman & Young, 1996; Kyle, 1997; Luster, Varelas, Wenzel & Liao, 1997; Smith, 1998). In the first of these studies (Luster et al., 1997), researchers investigated gendered discourse in a sixth-grade science class in Chicago, Illinois, USA. The class was composed predominately of African American students from low- and middle-income homes. In this class, girls dominated the discourse. Girls were involved in collecting data, making predictions, developing explanations, and working to understand scientific models in terms of their own experiences. The girls, more than the boys, were talking and writing about science in a way that showed their deeper understandings. Barbara Luster and her colleagues (1997) explained these findings in light of prior research that showed the gender gap to be far less in science between African American females and males than between European American females and males (Kahle & Rennie, 1993). The authors also attributed the females' successful participation to the teacher's efforts to make class discussion safe for females.

Sally Smith (1998) noted similar findings for middle school African American females in a literature-discussion group. Within the context of a racially diverse book-club discussion group, early adolescent girls were able to raise their own agenda and negotiate their issues and identities within the multiple subjectivities of race, age, and culture in same-sex grouping. African American females were vocal in the group. The girls, as well as their language arts teacher, reported similar behavior in classroom discussions. One African American female stated,

> I think the girls are better than the boys in terms of intelligence [snickers from several]. I'm not being funny about that, I'm serious, and so, we usually dominate the class, and the boys are just doing that to get attention, but we're busy answering the difficult and hard questions. (p. 8)

In explaining her findings, Smith reported that researchers suggest that middle-class African American females do not lose their voice and resist both gender and racial stereotypes because of a sense of competence and independence nurtured during adolescence by role models and an awareness of strong females in history (Haag, 1999). Other research suggests that when placed in predominately white classrooms, black females learn to silence their voices to become academically successful (Fordham, 1993).

Stacia Kyle (1997), an African American graduate student, also investigated African American students' discussions in a private school. She found that African American females dominated classroom discussions of romantic literature in a middle school class composed of 50% males and 50% females, most of whom were African Americans. She also observed African American girls helping to keep the boys on task and answering African American boys' academic questions. The teacher reported that this behavior was typical of the types of interactions in the class and characterized her African American female students as very expressive with dominating personalities. One African American female in the class referred to boys' participation in discussion as inattentive or argumentative, with females unafraid to dominate class discussions:

> Either they won't listen or they'll argue. They'll take it as me telling them a fact rather than an opinion. The guys usually don't participate unless it is controversial or unless they take offense to what we say. If the males are offended, they speak up, but if it is school related they are usually quiet. As a female though, I ain't intimidated by them at all. If you come at me, I'm comin' right back at cha. (pp. 8–9)

Kathleen Hinchman and Josephine Young (1996) similarly described an African American female who liked to argue (according to the student's self-perception and the perception of others), was outspoken, and got her point across in class discussions. She resisted other group members' attempts to silence her contributions to her eighth-grade language arts class discussions. Although her group members did not acknowledge or elaborate on her responses, she still verbally contributed her ideas despite this lack of recognition. She was able to remain an active and vocal participant, although over time, she eventually did become increasingly silent.

Discussion

Each of these studies illustrated one of five themes: (1) patterns of gendered discursive practice, (2) gendered talk in literature-response groups, (3) the stability of gendered discursive practice across content areas, (4) the difficulties and dangers of interrupting gendered discursive practices, and (5) the problem of essential-izing. In the first theme, patterns of gendered discursive practice, literacy researchers identified many of the same gendered discursive practices previously identified in studies by sociolinguists. These gendered practices (call outs, interruptions, teasing, and contradictions) that marginalized others usually were associated with males, although they could be characteristic of any students who hold inordinate power over others. This subset of studies offers a clear picture of these kinds of interactions that impede or facilitate females' (and some males') abilities to develop and express their ideas.

These studies are practically significant because students' understandings are formed and expressed by language, whether written or oral forms of language (Vygotsky, 1978). Some researchers (e.g., Almasi, 1995) demonstrated that students who were allowed to verbalize their ideas were able to experience conceptual change, leading to increased understandings of concepts and enabling students to locate and deal with conflicts between group members. Hence, it is important to be able to identify the ways in which students are marginalized by gendered interactions and what and how language behaviors disenfranchise others.

The second theme, gendered talk in literature-response groups, addressed issues of group composition. When left to their own devices, students in mixed-gender groups tended toward power imbalances in discussion. The social relations between group members tended to influence the quantity and types of participation by males and females. In addition, the practice of asking students to relate to the characters by putting themselves in the place of the character or recalling their own experiences that relate to the character's actions and feelings may serve to perpetuate gender stereotypes. In this interpretation of reader response, students are not taught to critically question gendered representations in text.

The third theme, the stability of gendered discursive practice across content areas, addressed the question of whether particular subject areas favor gendered language patterns. Together, the studies addressed the question of whether subjects like science, typically considered to be male dominated, would produce more gendered language patterns than a content area like language arts, often considered to be more of a female's domain. Research by Guzzetti and Williams (1996a, 1996b) showed that European American males in high school did indeed dominate science classes. Females tended to avoid refutational discussions that required debate of ideas, particularly in whole-class discussions. Other studies (Tolmie & Howe, 1993; Wilson & Haug, 1995) found that males were also more likely to argue for their views in subjects like science, English, and geography.

The fourth theme, the difficulties and dangers of interrupting gendered discursive practices, was illustrated in studies that went beyond documenting and describing gendered language patterns to attempting to intervene in the perpetuation of those practices. These studies showed that both teachers and students may not care to disrupt existing norms or gendered beliefs and practices. As these studies show, attempts to do so may actually reinforce those practices.

The final theme, the problem of essentializing, addressed the dangers inherent in simplistic characterizations of and solutions to gendered discursive practices in classrooms. Taken as a body, these studies show us that we cannot generalize (e.g, that all males talk one way and all females talk another), particularly because most of this research has focused exclusively on the behaviors of middle-class European American students. Through their identification of participants' race and social class, these studies make some attempt at recognizing the multiple layers people have that interact with gender.

Recommendations for Instruction

Many of these researchers provided recommendations for instructional practice. In this section, we provide the most common recommendations found in this research.

First, teachers may need to become action researchers in their own classrooms by active and systematic search for gender bias. Researchers suggest that most teachers are unaware of any gender inequities in their classrooms (Jones & Wheatley, 1990; Tobin, 1988). Even award-winning teachers who think that their own practices are gender fair may not be aware that their students' interactions with one another are not gender fair, and can be the greatest source of gender bias in the classroom (Guzzetti & Williams, 1996a, 1996b). It would seem, therefore, that the first step would be to become aware of students' gendered talk that marginalizes others. If teachers know what behaviors to look for, they can observe for them and become aware if these gendered language patterns exist in their own classrooms. These studies documented that students' behaviors such as interrupting, call outs, teasing, contradicting, using gaze aversion, ignoring responses, and dominating the conversational floor with number and length of turns all serve to disenfranchise others. Teachers can make checklists or matrixes and observe for these behaviors in students' small-group and whole-class discussions. Teachers can also design their own questionnaires to solicit students' observations and feelings regarding their own class discussions. In doing so, teachers can discover the social relations among students that influence their participation.

Second, teachers can involve students in identifying gendered discursive practices. Students can also observe for these behaviors by tracing participation patterns and recording frequencies and types of participation in small groups. In addition, teaching students discourse analysis techniques can also serve to heighten awareness of and change gendered language patterns. Students can be taught to track power relations through language by recording who makes assertions versus who tentatively questions, who gains the floor and who holds it, and whose comments get elaborated on and whose get dropped.

Third, talking about the discussion in classrooms between and among teacher and students may help to alleviate asymmetrical discussion patterns. If teachers or students find evidence of power imbalances in classroom discussion, several researchers (e.g., Edelsky & Harman, 1991; Gallas, 1995; Guzzetti & Williams, 1996a) have recommended that teachers and students metacommunicate, or talk about the talk in the classroom. By doing so, individuals may become aware of their own behaviors and may be helped to self-monitor themselves.

Fourth, teachers may wish to form small groups by gender for discussion, particularly when discussion of the text or topic favors males, requires debate, or may lead to embarrassment or ridicule. Several researchers found that female students had more opportunities and felt safer in participating when they were grouped on the basis of their sex. Other students, like the students in these studies, may also prefer to be grouped by gender.

Finally, teachers can see through these studies that there are both risks and benefits associated with attempts to change talk that marginalizes others. Teachers may be reminded that their efforts to change gendered talk may be met with some resistance. These studies have shown that those who enjoy power often do not enjoy relinquishing it (e.g., Alvermann, Commeyras, et al., 1997; Guzzetti & Williams, 1996a, 1996b). Those students who have been associated with less power, particularly females, may be reluctant to disturb the status quo because of fear of damaging their reputations as females and diminishing their popularity with the opposite sex.

Recommendations for Research

These studies provide five implications for both the report and conduct of future investigations in gender and literacies. These implications are drawn from the silences in the studies as well as the findings.

First, researchers should describe themselves and their prior experiences that may influence the conduct and analysis of their studies. Few investigators of the gender and discussion studies described themselves, specifically their ethnicities, social classes, or genders. Generally, researchers also were silent about their prior related experiences or personal beliefs that might influence the type of data they collected and the interpretation of those data. Only in rare cases did researchers refer to the ways in which they influenced the research or how the research influenced them. From the feminist framework we have chosen, this is problematic. For as Sandra Acker (1994) argues, authentic feminist research is not so much driven by a list of design criteria as it is an approach to research that is informed by a stance that clearly defines the researcher's position in relation to the world she or he seeks to understand. We are, therefore, reminded of Acker's query: Is all research done by feminists necessarily feminist research?

Second, researchers should conduct more studies that incorporate interviews with students to determine their perceptions and motivations. Studies also were rife with speculation about the intentions of students' language. In reading these studies, we wanted to be able to interview the students to determine their motivations and intentions. Too many studies relied on observation of but not interviews with students. Students have been shown to be articulate and capable of metacommunication, particularly at the middle and high school levels where most of this research was conducted (Guzzetti & Williams, 1996a).

Third, researchers should expand the scope of their samples. These researchers tended to limit their investigations to studies of middle-class European American students. This focus tends to perpetuate the belief that gender is fixed and stable and ignores the nuances of multiple subjectivities. When taken as a body, these studies reinforce the dangers of essentializing. Other researchers (Grant & Sleeter, 1986) also found that race, social class, and gender are treated as separate issues in the education literature, with little integration. Such studies lead to essentializing gender and to oversimplification of the analysis of students' behaviors. Hence, more studies are needed to describe how males and females of various cultural backgrounds, ethnicities, generations, geographies, and social classes interact in instructional settings.

Fourth, future researchers who do choose to investigate students of various races should become familiar with feminist frameworks that reflect the cultures they are studying. We noted, as did our external coders, that researchers who did study students of color usually did not choose to conduct their studies from frameworks representative of black or Latina feminisms. Rather, these researchers filtered their data collection and analysis from European American feminist perspectives. Until researchers expand the scope and frames of their investigations; explicate characteristics of their informants; describe themselves and their experiences prior, during, and after the research; and involve students more directly in addressing the issues of gendered discursive practices, the literature on gender and discussion will remain incomplete and limited.

Finally, we hope that future research will include more teacher partnerships and action research. The reports of participants' disinterest in addressing gendered discursive practices that researchers have noted may in be due in part to students' feelings of impotence and alienation (Edelsky & Harman, 1991). These researchers caution that when investigations are not tied to action, the result may be participants' disempowerment. They suggest that students investigate and critique their discourse, extending language-as-a-tool to language-as-a-topic to address the problem of alienation. Because metacommunication is offered as a way of involving students in resolving the problem, it also should be used as a method of data collection.

CHAPTER 3

Studies on Gender and Reading

Characteristics of the Studies

Thirty-eight studies explored the influence of gender on reading. The majority of these were conducted in the United States (66%), with 18% conducted in Canada, 11% in the United Kingdom, and 5% in Australia. Most of the first authors of the studies were female (87%) and European American (50%) also. Ethnicity had to be inferred on the basis of familiarity for 47% of first authors. Females also were most often second authors (24%) and third authors (8%). Males were 13% of first authors and 3% of second authors. The gender of 73% of second authors was not stated and could not be inferred. Most authors conducted their investigations from multiple theoretical frames of which 66% were critical literacy or some type of feminism (42%), such as poststructural feminism, socialist feminism, critical feminism, radical feminism, and unspecified forms of feminism. Literacy as a social practice also appeared in 29% of the studies, as did social constructivism (21%) and language as a social practice (8%). About one third of this research was case study, one third was qualitative; two thirds was published.

The studies focused on females only (39%) or included both males and females (21%), and 11% focused on males only. Gender was not stated in 29% of the studies. Most of the studies investigated adolescents (48%)—11% investigated junior high school students, 32% middle school, and 5% high school students; 3% were conducted with preschool children and 8% with primary students. At other grade levels, 18% of the studies were conducted with intermediate elementary students, 11% with graduate students, and 5% with adults.

A small number (8%) focused on a range of ages and social classes. Most studies investigated either middle-class students (41%) or middle- to upper-class students (21%), whereas 35% focused on lower socioeconomic-status students: working class (21%), working poor (11%), or poverty level (3%). Unlike studies from other areas, 76% of the authors stated their participants' social class.

Themes

Four themes resulted from our analyses of the literature on gender and reading:

1. importance of text and method in literature response
2. gendered reading preferences and practices
3. oppression or constraint in instructional and social context
4. opposition, accommodation, and resistance in reading

These themes are identified and exemplified in the following sections.

Importance of Text and Method in Literature Response

Concerns about literature response or reader response were addressed in 12 studies (Barrow, Broaddus, & Crook, 1995; Broughton, 1998; Cherland, 1992, also reported in 1994; Davies, 1991, 1993; Ferrell, 1998; Gonzalez, 1997; Hanley, 1998; Johnson, 1997; Johnson & Fox, 1998; Nauman, 1997; Pace & Townsend, 1999; Prosenjak, 1997). Meredith Cherland (1992, 1994) and Bronwyn Davies (1989) contended that the influence of gender must be considered as teachers implement reader response, particularly when reader-response theory is translated into practice as relatively unstructured responses to literature. These researchers believe that gender is a social construction, and reading is a social practice. When students are left to their own interpretations, they bring their understandings of gender and their lived experiences to their readings. These understandings are often limiting and stereotypical and do not assist students in deconstructing sexist (or racist or classist) messages in texts.

Davies (1993), an Australian researcher, illustrated these concerns. She conducted a follow-up study to her earlier study (1991) with primary students to determine any changes in these students' previously identified gendered responses to feminist fairy tales and fiction. During a year-long study with seven of the eight original children (three girls and four boys), stories were read to the children and discussed in literature-response groups. The children's reactions to these stories "illustrated the power of traditional storylines to assert oppressive gender relations as natural and correct" (p. 173). Davies found that these children displayed the same patterns as they did 4 years earlier. Those who disrupted gendered generalizations continued to do so, and those who perpetuated gendered categories also continued to do so.

Therefore, Davies (1993) criticized reader response because, in reader response, students put themselves in a character's place and relate their own feelings and experiences to those of the character. This process perpetuates gender stereotyping because the influence of gender, formed through experience, positions females and males to read texts differently. In reader response, students are not taught to read against the text or to challenge gender stereotypes. By not teaching students to take a critical stance, the teacher perpetuates existing gendered attitudes and behaviors. Davies advocated that teachers familiarize children with ways to deconstruct texts.

Like Davies, Cherland (1992, 1994) criticized reader response in a study of middle school readers in Canada. She observed sixth graders in reader-response groups that were formed as mixed- and same-gender groups. These groups conducted self-directed discussions of a book that all the students had read. Although Cherland chose the books and formed the groups, discussions were unstructured. Children in the literature-response groups were asked for their individual views of the book. Using the text for support, they worked alone and focused on their own responses.

In subsequent discussions, students enacted their understandings of gender during both the reading of fiction and in their talk about fiction. For example, when a female voiced a concern that a story was scary, a boy logically informed her that it was only a story, so she had no reason to be afraid. In another example, two boys in their comparisons of *Shane* (Schaeffer, 1981), a novel about a gunfighter, and *Tuck Everlasting* (Babbitt, 1986), a novel of a family that became immortal, praised *Shane* for its action, adventure, and realism and criticized the other novel for its lack of realism. In ways like these, boys were inclined more than girls to participate in a discourse of action by using reason and logic. Boys tended to define characters by what they did rather than by what they felt, seeking meaning in the plot and action of the story.

Conversely, girls responded to stories with a discourse of feeling. For example, Karen, a female student, described her feelings about an event in *Julie of the Wolves* (Craighead, 1972), which is a book about a 13-year-old girl who spends an Artic winter living with a wolf pack. In this story, a wolf from the pack is shot; Karen articulated her depression and sadness at this event and compared her feelings to those of the character in the story. In another instance, Karen stated that she could not love her brothers in the way the character, Sara, loved Charlie in *Summer of the Swans* (Byars, 1996), because Karen's brothers would not accept her love. In addition, other female students tended to identify the emotional states of the character with phrases such as, "That bothered her" or "she cared" (Cherland, 1992, p. 189). In these ways, girls were more inclined than boys to focus on emotion and human relationships in texts and, subsequently examined plots in terms of character development.

These students' reactions to stories also were gendered in other ways. For example, the children thought in terms of *boys' books* and *girls' books*. Not one boy would admit to ever having read a girl's book. These students considered reading, particularly reading fiction, to be a female activity. Their talk about these books also reflected patterns of gendered discussion (see Chapter 2) previously identified in the literature by researchers such as Tannen (1990).

Cherland (1992) suggested that the literature discussions were gendered because the students came into the group with their gendered cultural beliefs about how to engage in conversations, about human relationships, and their about what is of value in a story. Their discussions were unstructured; the goal was simply to talk about the book. This lack of structure allowed and encouraged the children to speak to each other in ways informed by their gendered beliefs.

Other studies did not criticize reader response as a method but demonstrated the limitations of unstructured responses to text in helping students deconstruct texts. These studies showed that how the ways in which readers' responses were facilitated were as important as the text was in defying gender stereotypes. In most cases, the ways in which literature groups were conducted were not described in detail, but were implied as relatively unguided by the teacher and characterized by students' free responses. For example, Nancy Prosenjak (1997) showed how readers responded to text when left to their own devices and demonstrated the need for teacher modeling of ways to approach texts that do not fit gender stereotypes. Prosenjak studied the reading responses of 22 middle school readers in two schools. She asked students to examine and discuss fiction with characters that either validated or challenged the experience of students' lives. Students were asked questions related to the realism of character portrayal and asked to share their reading strategies for dealing with characters they found unrealistic or unfamiliar. Prosenjak found that rather than examining the attributes that made the character different from themselves, readers tended to focus on attributes that made the character similar to themselves, their friends, or their family members. These students also expected gender consistency in the actions of characters, and some indicated that they would stop reading a book if the character's actions did not fit the character's gender. Others stated that they would shift their focus to a more likeable character or imagined other responses by the character when characters did not meet their perceptions of appropriate actions for a person of that gender.

Males and females were also gendered in the ways they read texts. Boys and girls read texts for different reasons and in different ways. Although girls sometimes admired the strong actions of a girl character, they still expected her to be a typical female in other ways. Girls almost always commented that they wanted to enter a story in a personal way. They tended to select books written about children, and most often selected books written for young females and their problems, or they selected mysteries. In contrast, boys selected adult books with adult men as characters more than they selected children's books. Boys read mainly for plot action, so they did not try to identify with the character and, therefore, did not focus on the character's actions that might be inappropriate for them as young boys.

Prosenjak (1997) concluded that these middle school readers responded to gendered texts in a gendered way. Because they brought their gendered expectations with them to the text, students detected gendered messages within the text. The researcher recommended that middle school readers be taught and encouraged to ask critical questions and to evaluate gendered stereotypes as they read. In a study of elementary, middle school, and college students' responses to literature (Barrow et al., 1995), it was also recommended that teachers examine their own responses to literature and take into account their students' experiences when considering their expectations for literature response.

Similarly, in a study of a first-year college literature class and an 11th-grade literature class, Barbara Pace and Jane Townsend (1999) found that biases against women were so embedded in the college students' perspectives as they engaged in reader-response groups that they were naturalized, as though they represented some universal truth. In the college classroom, the male teacher taught Shakespeare's *Hamlet* from the point of view of Hamlet, by assuming Hamlet's perspective and analyzing the play through Hamlet's eyes. The teacher looked for "right answers" and dominated discussions as the sole source of knowledge. Consequently, students voiced perceptions of the female and male characters (Gertrude and Hamlet) from patterns of thinking grounded in gender-role stereotypes. As the semester continued, students' voices became increasingly silent.

In the high school classroom, the female teacher demonstrated the power of teacher intervention through modeling and critical questioning. In this class, the teacher was not looking for a "right answer" and the students considered multiple perspectives in critical discussions of *Hamlet*. The study revealed that many students participated and voiced a variety of views about characters and the plot. The teacher's language about character interpretation was laced with uncertainty, which initiated a process of discovery with the students. The teacher modeled text referencing and critical questioning as ways of investigating literary meaning so that students could construct their own meanings. Consequently, the students' inquiry made the characters more human and complex in ways that made both stereotyping and traditional views of *Hamlet* problematic.

These differing responses to the same play indicated that the way in which students talk about characters and literature is as important as the characters and the literature that they talk about. Pace and Townsend (1999) argued, therefore, that "when students are encouraged to master processes of understanding, and when no single perspective is naturalized, both students and characters can escape gender role stereotypes" (p. 47). The authors agreed that the nature of discussion about a text and the methods for discussion were as critical as the text itself in dealing with gendered behaviors and perspectives.

When teachers structured reader response by selection of books and activities designed to promote critical questioning, literature study allowed for responses that reflected the myriad of possibilities of gender. For example, Heather Blair and Susan Reschny (1995) constructed a project loosely based on Rosenblatt's (1985) reader-response theory, and selected adolescent fiction featuring women in science fiction, historical fiction, and fantasy. The researchers met with four 9th-grade girls in a book club. In addition, the researchers observed a grade 7-8 class, who chose their book and group, read in class, discussed the books with each other, wrote in literature logs, and presented their books to the class. Students from both groups analyzed the main character from their book and discussed how they thought the author represented women in their novel.

The students generally liked the characters and found that they had strong characteristics, although they were not without faults. The women in historical fiction were often heroes. Although they were admired, the students made comments that the girls in these novels, like *Roll of Thunder, Hear My Cry* (Taylor, 1997) were atypical and exceptionally mature for their age. Realistic fiction provoked personal responses ranging from extreme dislike to empathy.

In a similar study, Bobby Lee Hanley (1998) examined how gender shapes reader response through case studies of two female and two male college students. Participants completed a reading interest questionnaire, wrote a reading autobiography detailing their histories as readers, maintained reader-response journals while reading, participated in interviews after reading each novel, responded to a follow-up survey based on questions that emerged from analysis of the interviews, and responded to the researcher's findings on them as readers.

Participants had responses illustrating four patterns. These included responses that identified the roles of females and males, responses that indicated a strong identification with characters of the same sex as the reader, responses that indicated a weak identification with characters of the opposite sex, and responses that recognized the patriarchal nature of the story world. An example of the patriarchal nature of novels came from a female student, Abby, who remarked that if a man had written *Jacob Have I Loved* (Paterson, 1980), there would not have been as much of a focus on family relationships. Both males and females identified books that were intended for males (with male characters) or for females (with female characters). For example, two informants, John and Debra, both agreed that the novel was a book for females with its emphasis on female characters and feelings. Readers were also gendered in how they read the novels. Female readers made personal connections to the characters and reacted emotionally to the story. Male readers were attracted to action and adventure and showed less emotion in their responses.

Hanly concluded by recommending that student teachers be trained to develop greater sensitivity to the sociocultural and political dimensions of texts and to examine the potential impact of texts they select for their students. Hanley cautioned that teachers must continue to gain understanding of both overt and covert messages conveyed in texts regarding race and gender. Teachers' instructional strategies should seek to counteract stereotypes and rewrite stereotypical stories.

Holly Johnson (1997) studied the reading responses of 11 adolescent girls aged 12 to 14 from diverse ethnic, racial, class, and religious backgrounds. These girls read novels of realism and social issues, as well as contemporary fiction, allowing for a comparison of female representation across genres. Participants voiced their responses in mixed-gender literature circles conducted by the researcher. The students elaborated on their responses in questionnaires and interviews in which they were asked consciousness-raising questions about females' roles and representations in realistic novels, about class and race representation, and about their own connections to the situations and to female characters within the novels.

Students' implicit ideologies were apparent in responses that included gender stereotyping, classism, and racism. These girls had narrow views on what it meant to be normal—female characters outside the norm of affluence and popularity, particularly those who were insecure, were not acceptable. Johnson concluded by recommending that teachers instruct students to challenge these gendered norms and interrogate the self as part of instruction.

April Nauman (1997) studied 21 sixth graders in a suburban elementary school for 4 months. Data were collected through classroom observations of and participation in small-group discussions, interviews, and literature-response journals. The purpose of the study was to determine how boys and girls related to and understood fictional characters, and how fictional characters influenced girls' and boys' perceptions of themselves and each other.

Nauman's study revealed several gendered patterns. Students reported that they related best to fictional characters who were similar to them in life experiences, values, personality, and gender. Most girls and virtually all boys wanted to read books about characters of their own sex, because students felt better able to understand same-sex characters and because of perceived differences between books about girls and about boys. Girls' books tended to be about relationships— friendships and romances and relationship problems; boys' books tended to be about adventure and fantasy. Girls' characters, tending to be identified as friends, served as models for how to solve real-life problems; the boys' characters, exhibiting high degrees of independence and ability, served as models of power.

Therefore, fiction that was approached uncritically became an important enculturating mechanism by which males and females learned traditional gender roles; that is, males were enculturated as adventurers, females as relationship tenders. Nauman (1997) concluded by advising that teachers choose students' books critically and encourage students to find ways of relating to characters that seem unlike them, which provides students with a chance to expand their sense of self and understanding of others.

Holly Johnson and Dana Fox (1998) studied 16 girls and 10 boys (12 Mexican American and 14 European American) in an eighth-grade class. The study focused on observations of and in-depth interviews with 17 students, particularly two girls who were passionate about their own value and sense of worth. The purpose of the study was to describe how young female students choose texts, what types of protagonists they choose, what their observations are of those characters, and how these female students accept or resist the messages of texts.

Two Anglo-American girls, Gillian and Angie, were chosen as case studies because they defied stereotypes and were unafraid to speak their minds. Gillian declared herself a feminist. Both longed for female characters more like them and wanted more "multilayered" people. Unlike other girls in the study, Gillian and Angie sought strong female characters. Some of the Mexican American and one of the

European American girls in the study saw female characters they found in young adult literature as "good enough" (p. 30).

Johnson and Fox proposed that teachers reconsider and rethink their own roles in teaching and learning literature. Teachers need to be fully vested participants in literature discussions, by offering their own responses to texts and their critiques of characters' motives and authors' story lines. Teachers should also make informed choices of literature that exposes students to a variety of cultures, or stories students may not have chosen to read on their own. Johnson and Fox concluded that students should be taught conceptual strategies to enable them to make multiple interpretations of texts and explore how those interpretations occur.

Jennifer Danridge (1999) conducted another study that demonstrated the importance of the text in literature response. Danridge was a participant observer in a book club composed of four African American women who were doctoral students in education. The discussion of a participant-selected book, Tony Morrison's *Song of Solomon* (1987), written by a black author about black characters, was audiorecorded and analyzed for the study. The purpose of the study was to describe how students in a book club talk about their cultural and literate identities that are under construction and explore the connections between identity, culture, and literacy.

Danridge found that the author provided African American readers with "a hope that we can find ourselves if we keep searching and looking and watching and listening" (p. 10). It was that message that motivated students to continue reading despite the fact that text was "hard to get into" or that "they didn't perceive themselves as avid readers" (p. 10). Danridge read the book twice, once from the point of view of the author and again from the perspective of one of the characters, attempting to put herself in the character's his place. Another participant, Tara, realized that Morrison rooted the characters in African American history and commented, "Morrison was trying to tell our history" (p. 10). Monique, another participant, remarked that she could relate to the story because it could have been the story of her neighbors or the family of someone she knew. Danridge noted that for many African Americans, stories like these have been lost or fragmented because slaves were not allowed to learn to read and write. Hence, these participants were able to relate to the author's message. The female characters in the book helped the participants examine their own cultural and gendered identities through discussions of their values, beliefs, and behaviors in relation to the characters' portrayals. Danridge concluded that the content of the book is critical to the level of personal connection and engagement that the reader experiences. In another study, Mary Broughton (1998) also noted the importance of the text to Hispanic girls who read *Lupita Mañana* (Beatty, 1981) in a book club and used this fictional story to examine their own lives.

Norma Linda Gonzalez (1997) reported similar findings in her study of European American, middle-class women in a book club. Gonzalez found that when females were grouped homogeneously by background and values to discuss favorite texts, they were comfortable to enough to speak freely. Hence, Gonzalez questioned the practice of literature discussions that group together children with diverse socioeconomic, cultural, and linguistic backgrounds to discuss a book selected from among the teacher's choices.

Gendered Reading Preferences and Practices

Sixteen studies conducted in the United States, Australia, Canada, and the United Kingdom examined social and pedagogical influences on females' and males' reading choices, behaviors, and responses (Benjamin & Irwin-DeVitis, 1998; Blair & Sanford, 1999; Brown, 1997; Cherland, 1994; Christian-Smith, 1993a; Dressman, 1997; Ferrell, 1998; Finders, 1996; Gonzalez, 1997; Mallett, 1997; Millard, 1994, 1997; Osmont, 1987; Rice, 2000; Silliman, 1997; Willinsky & Hunniford, 1993). For example, Elaine Millard (1994) observed and interviewed 10- and 12-year-old students prior to implementation of the National Curriculum in Britain. She discovered that school reading was more pertinent to the interests of girls than to boys and showed gender disparities in instructional reading practices. For example, the majority of books read in classrooms were narrative texts. Boys preferred nonfiction books, magazines, or comic books that were not available to them. Reading was a time filler, and there was little monitoring of free reading, which resulted in the struggling readers (usually boys) continuing with patterned texts and not expanding their interests. Students seldom saw the purpose of reading in school.

These findings prompted Millard (1997) to expand her study by surveying 225 students and interviewing 16 of those students to further determine their perceptions of and practices in reading. The findings confirmed the gender differences found in her initial study. The social practices of the school and those of the wider community worked together to create a context in which reading contributed to establishing dichotomous gender identity. For example, students' comments in interviews demonstrated that from an early age, reading was identified as an activity of females. Children of both sexes designated their mothers and other female relatives as models for reading. In addition, children saw their mothers and fathers differently as readers. Mothers read to them or with them. Fathers may have read, but they read for work-related reasons or for a specific purpose, such as searching for information. Girls were more likely to receive books as presents than boys were, and book illustrations more often portrayed girls as readers. Most girls identified themselves as readers and book lovers, most boys did not. Girls read more than boys did, and girls read for personal enjoyment. Boys read primarily in school and for assignments. Girls talked about books to friends or female family members. These discussions were an established part of their social life. Conversely, boys did not like to talk about reading or about books. Boys and girls also remembered learning to read and reading in school differently. Most boys remembered little about learning to read. Those who did remember said that it was not easy for them; however, girls remembered well the process of learning to read and looked back on it as enjoyable. Millard concluded that families and schools play a critical role in developing children's attitudes, preferences, and success in reading. A family's belief system surrounding reading, particularly their beliefs about which kinds of reading are appropriate for male or female family members, influences young readers.

Studies conducted by other researchers confirmed Millard's findings by exploring influences on boys' perceptions of and practices in reading (Blair & Sanford, 1999; Osmont, 1989; Wheeler, 1984). For example, Heather Blair and Kathy Sanford (1999) conducted a study at a large junior high school located in a white suburb in Canada. They asked how boys saw themselves as literate and asked what schools did and did not do that affected boys' views of and performance in reading by observing seventh- and eighth-grade classes and interviewing students, teachers, and administrators. The researchers also conducted surveys of literacy practices, reading inventories, and reading profile interviews with nine seventh-grade boys.

The same patterns were found by Blair and Sanford that were found by Millard (1994, 1997). Learning to read had been difficult for many of the boys. Boys defined reading in narrow terms: reading was school-related and consisted of teacher-selected texts, such as novels, short stories, or poetry. Boys felt no personal sense of purpose or pleasure in reading. The consensus among boys was that they did not like to read. Individual comments included, "I've never read a book that I liked," "I'm not really a reader, so how can I love reading?" and "In a movie, you get to see things, right? A book, you have to imagine it, and you have to read it, and I don't like it" (Blair & Sanford, 1999, p. 6). Boys reported that it was not cool to read a long novel or to talk to other boys about books. They preferred visual media—the Internet, nonfiction, newspapers, or magazines—that focused on sports, electronics, and games, most of which were not found in their classrooms. These boys discounted their choices as reading because their preferred texts were not a part of their school's reading program. Mark Dressman (1997) discovered similar reading preferences in his study of third-grade students' practices in three school libraries. His observations revealed that females typically searched the library's fiction section, whereas boys checked out nonfiction.

Peggy Rice (2000) asked European American and African American sixth graders in a middle- to upper middle-class community to read a feminist folk tale and recall it immediately afterward and again in 2 months. The analysis showed that females had twice as many inclusions of nontraditional gender roles in their written recalls than did males. Rice concluded that males and females did not alter a dualistic perception of maleness and femaleness, although females indicated some movement away from gender stereotypes. Males appeared to be especially restricted by their notions of masculine and feminine positions and qualities.

Similarly, Joan Ferrell (1998) conducted a study with her community college students to determine the role that gender plays in interpretation of texts. Students read stories that addressed marriage, adultery, and husband and wife roles. Despite written reflections and discussions, males were less likely than females to change their initial sympathies for the characters. Ferrell speculated that perhaps males might more readily rethink their interpretations of text if they were placed in small groups for discussion with males only.

The issue of what boys or girls read and how they interpret text also has been a focus for researchers who investigated girls' reading attitudes and practices. Researchers explored young females' attraction to young adult novels, popular romance fiction, and magazines such as *Sassy, Seventeen,* and *YM* (Benjamin & Irwin-DeVitis, 1998; Cherland & Edelsky, 1993; Christian-Smith, 1993a, 1993b; Finders, 1996; Willinsky & Hunniford, 1993). These studies highlighted the ways in which gendered subjectivities are constructed and reconstructed through interactions with these texts. For example, Beth Benjamin and Linda Irwin-DeVitis (1998) reported that sixth-, seventh-, and eighth-grade adolescent girls defined the ideal female character as one who is smart, but does not argue or voice her opinion. Girls identified being liked, being nice, and maintaining relationships as traits of favorite female characters. Girls chose female characters as ideals because these characters were nurturing and self-sacrificing.

In a similar way, Linda Christian-Smith (1993a, 1993b) examined how teen romance novels constructed the gender, class, racial, ethnic, and sexual subjectivities of 29 middle- and working-class young women, ages 12 through 15, from diverse racial and ethnic backgrounds. The researcher studied these readers for 8 months in two outlying middle schools and one inner-city junior high school located in a large midwestern U.S. city. Christian-Smith used interviews with teachers and librarians and her personal reviews of book orders and checkout cards to find girls who were habitual romance-fiction readers. Using these means, she found and surveyed 75 girls; from questionnaire survey results, she selected 29 girls to observe in language arts classes and interviewed the girls and their teachers.

Christian-Smith found that European American teenage girls were the most avid readers of romance novels; fewer African American, Hispanic American, or Asian American girls read these kinds of novels. Teachers and librarians characterized the girls who were the heaviest readers of romance fiction as reluctant or slow readers who were in low-level courses and were barely passing their subjects. These teachers were uncomfortable with allowing the girls to read romance fiction. Two European American teachers, one from a middle school on the outskirts of the city and one from a school in the inner city, commented that although romance novels had simplistic story lines and were full of stereotypes, they were pleased that the girls were at least reading and that their classrooms were quiet when students read.

These girls sought romance novels as an escape from teacher-selected books, which they considered boring, long, and irrelevant to their lives. One girl commented,

> I read a story about a girl stranded on this island and how she survives [Perhaps Scott O'Dell's (1990) *Island of the Blue Dolphins*]. It was interesting, but it doesn't have much to do with my life. Get real! How many girls are stranded on islands in 1985? At least with Sweet Valley, the stories are fun and I learn a lot about boys. (Christian-Smith, 1993a, p. 51)

The girls resisted assigned reading by complaining about the stories and mutilating book pages and covers. They also went to the classes' reading area and "covertly read their favorite romances, which they had stashed among the floor cushions" (Christian-Smith, 1993a, p. 51). Romance novels helped them to turn around what they considered to be a tedious day at school or problems at home. In this way, romance reading was pleasurable and engaging, because it depicted a world that was an ideal for the girls. These females often remarked that they put themselves in the place of a character or became the heroine. They experienced positive feelings about themselves as they read, and "Being recognized as someone special, with the qualities of niceness, intelligence, and humor was important to these young women" (p. 53).

These girls were well aware of their academic position and wanted their teachers and other adults to view them as nice and smart, despite their academic performance and placement. The girls also saw romance novels as a guide for interacting with boys (Christian-Smith, 1993a). The novels provided what the girls thought was valuable information about romance, particularly for girls whose parents forbade them to date. The novels provided a comfort zone for the girls where they could find out about romance without taking risks. For the girls, a satisfying romance novel had to be easy to read and action packed, and had to end happily. The hero and the heroine each had to be cute, smart, popular, nice, and have money. The girls thought that the boys they knew did not measure up to the ideal shown in romance novels. They hoped for a boyfriend who was sensitive to their needs and feelings, like the heroes they read about. They believed that a boy and a girl should resolve difficulties and their romance should end happily, not only in the stories, but in their lives as well. Girls also admired heroines who were assertive and strong, particularly toward boys, and showed great pleasure in reading about heroines who "got the best of boys" (p. 55). This notion of "besting boys" and "keeping them in line" occurred in situations where the heroine knew best, when the hero was treading on "female things" or trying to compel the heroine to do things against her beliefs. Girls were less confident about taking similar action in their own lives, however.

The novels had other effects on the girls' beliefs and behaviors. For example, a tug-of-war between the girls' views of conventional femininity and more assertive behaviors, like standing up to boys, characterized their reading of romance novels. Their social-class positions were reinforced as they read these novels. Their views of work, marriage, and children concomitantly fed into their reading of romance fiction. Because of the consumerist nature of the books and their emphasis on material things, appearance, and popularity as tickets to romance, all the girls worked to earn money for clothes and makeup.

John Willinsky and R. Mark Hunniford (1993) also discovered that adolescent females used romance novels as instruction manuals to guide their behavior with boys. In their study, seventh-grade girls from working-class homes in Canada liked heroines who were intelligent, had a sense of humor, and were beautiful. They also preferred strong, virile male heroes. These girls did not see the importance of independence in their characters

Cherland (1992, 1994) conducted a study with similar findings about girls' readings of fiction. She observed seven sixth-grade girls in an affluent white suburb in western Canada. Cherland observed the girls in their classroom, interviewed the girls' teacher and parents, and conducted a literature study with a small group of the girls. She found that these girls used their self-selected reading of the Sweet Valley High and Babysitters' Club series combatively, as an escape from being good, and to resist the demands of school and home. Their reading of fiction also helped to establish their social relationships with other girls, assisted them in emulating their mothers, and led them to explore agency or being active participants with choices in their lives and their literacies.

Influences of the larger culture, however, placed these girls in a passive position. Like the girls in Christian-Smith's study, these girls admired heroines who were assertive and independent in ways that they could not be. As Cherland (1994) stated, "They used reading to explore alternative ideas, both about agency and about gender" (p. 177). In this respect, reading served as a compensatory activity, a way to feel more powerful, and a means to shape and validate their values of consumerism, appearance, and popularity.

The girls in Margaret Finders's (1996) study read teen magazines or "'zines" in similar ways to those girls who read romance fiction in the Cherland and Christian-Smith studies. Finders conducted an ethnographic study at a midwestern U.S. junior high school. She observed and followed four early-adolescent girls, including two sets of self-proclaimed best friends and their larger circle of friends. Her observations encompassed their sixth-grade year through their completion of seventh grade. Finders wanted to document literacy events from the girls' point of view and to make visible the tacit rules and demands that shaped literacy and social roles within these particular social networks.

Finders observed that there were clearly demarcated social groups of girls in the school. The group who did not read 'zines was known as the "tough cookies." Another group called the "social queens" became the principal focus of the study because it was evident that the group members used 'zines as a marker for measuring how they were progressing into womanhood. Possession of a 'zine served as a sign of crossing the boundary from childhood into adolescence. Reading or just carrying a 'zine marked the girls as cool and as an insider and separated them from classmates who they viewed as kids not ready to deal with women's stuff.

Girls read these magazines as an exclusive social activity, which signified a select status and places other girls as outsiders. They read 'zines as instructional manuals or references for desired experiences and appearances, commenting on every page. Whoever got the magazine first for the month had the highest status among the girls. The girls considered the magazines to be exclusively theirs, and read them in a private place, away from adult judgments. The girls were proud that their parents and teachers disapproved of reading teen magazines, and that they were able to defy them. Although the girls perceived romance and sexuality as appropriate adult behavior, they kept the magazines away from adults because they deemed their conversations about them to be too "gross" for adults.

Because 'zines were not considered legitimate literature by teachers and were not condoned in the classroom, there was no critical discussion of the information in them with the teacher. Therefore, girls continued to accept information from articles and advertisements equally as truth. Finders (1996) noted that when one mother commented to her daughter that she was uncomfortable with the teen magazines because the ads were too sensual, her daughter replied as she turned a magazine's pages, "What advertisements?" (p. 82). These girls accepted the narrow life choices for females implicit in the articles and advertisements. They attributed authority to the teen magazines and used them to define their emerging roles in society. They identified with a traditional notion of womanhood projected by the magazines, one that was rooted in a consumerist culture, and in unquestioning acceptance of the centrality of males to their lives. Finders warned, "These messages read over and over become scripts for the girls and will be impossible to revise unless they are made visible" (p. 83).

In addition to teen magazines, other genres were stereotypically female choices as well. For example, Bessy Silliman (1997) explained the appeal of horror fiction to 13- and 14-year-old girls. She found that both the texts and the readers' responses reflected white, middle-class ideologies and models of gender and sexually appropriate behaviors. These novels demonstrated an absence of gender-challenging females. Rather than resist these images, female adolescents were attracted to the feelings of horror aroused in them by death, flesh, and blood.

Other genres typically attracted young male readers. For example, Jeffrey Brown (1997) investigated comic book readers in Canada and found, as Mallett (1997) did in the United States, that preadolescent and adolescent boys are the primary readers of comic books. Brown interviewed boys at specialty stores, shopping malls, and comic book conventions and found that stereotypical gender divisions regarding purposes for reading (e.g., women read for social reasons, and men read for facts) was inaccurate. The young males in his study read comic books to satisfy a social function, reading for a sense of community, with either the characters and the narrative world, or with other comic book fans. These black and white males formed a textual community by holding regular meetings of their comic book club, sharing books with each other, and discussing characters' traits and actions. Observations of these meetings revealed that the boys had immense emotional involvement with the characters they followed. Boys read comic books to gain prestige among other boys (as Finders [1996] found with girls who read teen magazines to gain prestige with each other), to feel a sense of kinship or continuity with favorite characters and comic book artists, to emulate moral codes of conduct, to find constant friends and comfort in a world of family turmoil, or to learn what a male should be in either white or black culture by reading about comic characters of those races.

Analysis of these comic characters revealed the gendered nature of the comic book superhero. Brown found comic book superheroes to be clear representations of society's notions of masculinity—men who are powerful, tough, independent, resourceful, and dashing—the epitome of what society tells boys they should be. Brown (1997) observed, "The comic book model of masculinity asks what young reader wouldn't rather be a Superman than a mild-mannered Clark Kent" (p. 181). To one informant, Steve, reading comic books was an assertion of his own identity, a masculine identity that helped him gain his own space in a female-dominated home:

> I think one of the reasons I like comics so much right now is because my mom and my sister hate them. I always have to watch what they want on TV, listen to the music they want to listen to, and stuff. Neither one of them likes comics, so it's one of the few things that are my own. Only guys read comics, it's a man's thing. They are all about guys and they're for guys so…uh…women wouldn't know how to behave in a comic, anyway… they'd probably just panic and stuff. Like my friend David says, "it's men doing manly things…. If my Mom is fussing about my clothes not matching or being wrinkled, I'll say something like, "Well, you know, Mom, I don't think Batman would worry too much about his clothes." (p. 162)

These boys complained that teachers and parents did not appreciate the boys' reading comic books. One boy, Thomas, however, described his experience in second grade when his teacher had comic books and encouraged him to read them:

I always thought it was so cool that he would let us read comics in school, not a lot of teachers would allow that. In fact, I remember him letting me take some of the comics home so that I could become a better reader. It's not that I was stupid or anything; I just wasn't all that great a reader. I think I was bored by all those little kiddie books they made us read most of the time. Anyway, I really got into the comics he had and began reading them every day; by the end of the year I tested the highest in the class for reading skills. I was reading stuff that was meant for kids in the fifth grade. While other kids were just playing video games or listening to music, I was reading things. I don't care what people may say about comics being stupid; they're not. In fact, they're a lot more sophisticated than some of the stuff they used to make us read. If I'm a good student, and I am, it's 'cause of comics. (p. 154)

Brown's findings were supported by Pip Osmont's (1987) research. Osmont, an infant-school teacher in London, England, observed and interviewed teachers and students in two classrooms. Boys were enthusiastic about superhero books and comics and requested them in their classrooms. As a result, the teacher provided superhero comics, which children, particularly struggling readers, sat and read like newspapers. Osmont stated, "The gap between school views of children's literature and the children's books found in homes and High Street shops is often a very wide one, and I try to have a book collection that can include both" (p. 761).

Oppression or Constraint in Instructional and Social Context

Five studies identified oppressive conditions that constrained students' reading choices and practices in social or instructional contexts (Bardsley, 1999; Beach, 1995; DeBlase-Trzyna, 1999; Rigg, 1985; Wheeler, 1984). Doreen Bardsley (1999) conducted a study that illustrated both social and instructional constraints that produced gendered reading practices by exploring what reading fiction meant to sixth-grade boys in an urban middle school in the southwestern United States. Students were mostly European Americans, but the school, located in an upper middle-class neighborhood, also included Hispanic American and African American students. Bardsley selected four boys as her focal group, and conducted a literature study with them during their language arts class. She asked the boys to choose one book they wanted to read from the ones their teacher had presented in book talks. The boys read each book in three parts and discussed each part afterward, as well as reading aloud parts of it to each other. Bardsley also interviewed the boys, their teacher, and the boys' parents.

The reading practices of these boys, both in and out of school, were influenced by constraints that evolved from beliefs and practices of school personnel, their families, and their peers, as well as society in general. In school, the teacher selected books for guided and independent reading from a district-approved list. Students were not allowed to bring reading materials from home. They read fiction for most of the academic year and read nonfiction only during the last quarter of the year. The teacher also determined the pace of assignments for students' reading and followed reading with student work in journals and quizzes. Each student's parents were required to sign a weekly report to verify that they had seen their child's reading grades for that week.

During their reading and language arts time, the boys in the class usually wanted to choose their own books for reading and the length of time they would discuss them. Boys and girls had few opportunities, however, because in-school reading time was often shortened or interrupted by schedule demands. Within Bardsley's literature study group, however, the boys discussed books and collaborated successfully to make meaning of what they read. They readily and confidently responded to their reading because of a supportive environment in which they were able to make choices and decisions about their reading.

Nevertheless, the attitudes of both the boys and their parents' worked against boys' reading. For example, boys shared beliefs that reading was work, reading fiction was a school task, and reading was not fun. Reading was a requirement for the adult's world of work and for the child's world of school assignments. Parents who regarded reading and going to school as their child's job supported this view. Although these parents encouraged their boys to read more, they did not communicate that reading was enjoyable. The boys focused on sports and social activities outside of school, and those activities left them no time to read. Not having time to read was considered a status symbol because it meant that the boys were achieving success at something that was valued highly—sports.

Parents' pride in their sons' involvement in sports and social activities encouraged the boys' continued participation in them but discouraged boys' reading.

Mary Alice Wheeler (1985) observed similar patterns in her own fourth-grade son and his friends. The impetus for her study came from a comment made by the mother of one of the boys that her son and her friend's son were not reading anymore. This realization was difficult for the mothers to understand because they and their husbands had read to their sons from an early age, and they had modeled reading at home. In addition, there was always a variety of texts available in their homes, and they made weekly trips to the library. Wheeler conducted classroom observations and interviews of the boys and their mothers to determine why these boys had stopped reading.

Wheeler discovered that competing gendered interests was impeding the boys' reading. The boys' highest priority was sports. Their growing interest in sports was supported by their fathers, their peers, and in some cases, unknowingly by their mothers. There was an ever-present pressure for the boys to act and be "identifiably boys in public" (p. 613). This pressure affected the boys' choice of clothing, their verbal and body language, and their interests. Mothers tacitly encouraged this growing masculinity and separation with comments about not liking sports and not being able to talk to their sons about sports, thereby implicitly labeling sports as a male undertaking and consequently, more important for males than reading.

Like the participants in the studies by Blair and Sanford (1999), the boys in Wheeler's study did not read novels. Rather, they regularly read the sports news and the comics in their newspapers, information in their Cub Scout manual, assignments for Sunday school worksheets, and statistics on baseball cards. Mothers felt a loss as their sons moved away from the shared reading times they once experienced together to the kinds of reading activities engaged in by their fathers.

Teachers and mothers in Wheeler's study did not count the boys' use of their own preferred texts as reading. Teachers valued only what they assigned in school and for homework as reading. The boys did not consider what they were doing to be reading, either. Yet they were immersed in print encounters and were actually using a variety of texts. The question then became, What should count as reading—either at home or at school?

Richard Beach (1995) identified constraints of cultural models within peer groups as limiting both males' and females' responses to text. Beach asked 10th-grade students in two advanced and two regular English classes in a suburban high school to read and respond to the story by Richard Peck (1989), *I Go Along*. This is a story of a boy from a regular English class who chooses to attend a poetry reading attended by students in advanced English class. In the story, a female student from the advanced class befriends the boy. Male students' responses to this story reflected the assumption that the male experience is the norm or neutral standard against which female experience is judged, and being popular is achieved through competing with others, a belief derived from boys' experiences in sports. Females' responses reflected a different cultural model, which consisted of interpersonal effectiveness and resistance to partriarchal attitudes. These students unknowingly were constrained in their responses to text by the values of their peer groups.

Pat Rigg (1985) conducted another study that identified social as well as cultural constraints on literacy development. Rigg and a graduate student, Clara, attempted to teach a 45-year-old Mexican woman, Petra, a migrant worker, to read and write. Although Petra asserted her right to literacy by telling Rigg, "People like you should come to help me...at least to write my name" (p. 130), and she did accomplish this goal, Petra's further efforts to obtain the help she needed were impeded by her family's perception of her role as a Mexican female. Transportation to the public library for tutoring became an issue because Petra's 18-year-old son, José, had to drive her because the town had no bus service, and Clara had no car. As Rigg explained,

> This meant that when José finished his English class, he had to drive 5 miles home, pick up his mother, drive her the 5 miles back, babysit his 10-year-old brother for an hour and a half, and, finally, drive everyone back home. José preferred to work on the family car, which only he knew how to drive or was licensed to drive, or meet a couple of his buddies downtown. Petra was middle aged, a female, and most of all, she was his mother. José saw no reason for her to start reading and writing: better she stay home and make fresh tortillas for his arrival home from class. (p 137)

Rigg concluded,

> As an academic, I had read and talked about how one's literacy devel-
> opment is affected by the people with whom one most closely associates,
> and by the assumptions and expectations held by those people. Petra
> showed me what that really meant: It meant José's inability to remember
> that his mother had a reading lesson that day; it meant Petra's quiet ac-
> ceptance of being forgotten and waiting for a ride that never came. The
> context of Petra's family, especially the assumptions held by her son as
> to what was proper for a Mexican mother, almost denied her any litera-
> cy training. (p. 138)

Like Rigg, Gina DeBlase-Trzyna (1999) also told a story of oppression in describing an instructional climate that distanced adolescent females from their own lives in their interactions with literacy.
DeBlase-Trzyna observed and interviewed students in an eighth-grade
English classroom in a Native American magnet school to understand
how urban girls' constructions of social identities emerged from their
negotiations with texts. The researcher sought to provide insights
into how transactions with literacy contribute to the construction of
gendered worldviews and produce representations of gendered identity. To do so, she focused on 11 girls of European American, Native
American, Puerto Rican, and biracial (African American/Puerto Rican
and Native American/Puerto Rican) ethnicities.

Because of the teacher's authoritarian style and a teacher-centered
interpretation of text, the girls were never taught how to read from a
critical perspective or to resist the authority and values embedded
in text. For example, when reading a poem portraying love as
encompassing the light of the stars and the sun, one girl, Gabriella,
responded, "That don't sound right," and "It don't make any sense"
(DeBlase-Trzyna, 1999, p. 69), but the teacher never allowed her to
voice her ideas about the poem beyond that initial reaction.
In an interview with the researcher, Gabriella was able to convey that
she did not believe in love because it brought "a whole lot of broken
hearts and memories, and I don't like reminiscing on anything"
(p. 69). In the classroom, however, Gabriella's perspective on romantic love, grounded in her experience, was silenced and never considered. In another instance, the teacher asked Gabriella to ignore a
note passed by Lena, another student. To these girls, passing the note

represented engagement with the literature, and so it was an appropriate transaction. When the teacher realized Gabriella was writing a response to the note, she physically approached her, so Gabriella put the note under a book. When the teacher left her, Gabriella pulled out the note and continued to write. DeBlase-Trzyna (1999) concluded,

> The message was implicit, but very clearly sent between teacher and student, and the line was firmly drawn. To Mary, reading and writing notes, regardless of content, were not an appropriate enactment of literacy in the classroom. For Lena and Gabriella, the literacy transaction could be seen as their way of connecting classroom text to their own lives. In ways like these, girls in the class began to internalize that the price for academic success involved muting their own voices and accommodating the status quo. (p. 124)

Therefore,

> [T]here was little if any chance for the girls to make intertextual links to their own lived stories because knowledge, understanding, and knowing did not emerge from the classroom talk, and the teacher was perceived as not valuing students' experience of community knowledge. (p. 124)

Opposition, Accommodation, and Resistance in Reading

While reading fiction, females and males negotiate meaning as they engage with a text's depiction of gendered expectation and behaviors, and as they draw from their own contexts, experiences, and perceptions. Readers may accommodate the text by conforming to the gender roles represented in a text, or they may resist text by questioning those roles and arrive at their own interpretations and meanings. Five studies focused on opposition, accommodation, and resistance in reading (Cherland & Edelsky, 1993; Christian-Smith, 1993a, 1993b; Flynn, 1983; Wing, 1997) and opposition to school reading (Leroy, 1995).

Elizabeth Flynn (1983) expanded on notions of accommodation and resistance by viewing reading as a confrontation between self and text. She asserted that the reader can resist alien thoughts or subjects in text and dominate the text; therefore, the reader is detached and unchanged. Or, the reader can allow alien thoughts to replace his or her own and allow the text to dominate. Another possibility is that the reader and text interact in a mutual dialogue, so that the reader learns from reading without losing distance from the text. Flynn found that men in her freshman composition course showed dominance in their responses by failing to empathize with characters, detaching themselves emotionally, or dismissing a text entirely. In effect, they resisted the text. Conversely, women were better able to achieve a balance between attachment and involvement.

Alexis Wing (1997) explored a different kind of resistance by observing British 10- and 11-year olds' readings and discussions of *Bill's New Frock* (Fine, 1989), the story of a boy who wakes up one day to find that he has been changed into a girl and is wearing a pink dress. The children could not conceive of a boy wearing a dress but could not explain why. The girls thought it was insulting that Bill was referred to as "dear" when perceived as a boy; the boys thought it was unjust that Bill as a boy was reprimanded for certain behavior, but was not reprimanded for the same behavior as a girl. Children's discussions tried to focus on ways that adults treat boys and girls differently, but the discussions were constrained by the boys trying to control the discussions by shouting out reactions and mumbling during girls' comments. These children showed their understandings of teachers' expectations that girls be passive, responsible, and well behaved, while boys can be active, strong, untidy, and fight and express anger. These cultural expectations limited students' interpretations of text.

Like Wing, Cherland and Edelsky (1993) reexamined Cherland's (1992) observations of sixth-grade girls' reading in New Town, a suburb in western Canada, to study cultural reproduction and resistance. The researchers examined how the girls explored the possibilities of agency in fiction, and how they resisted roles that their parents envisioned for them, as exemplified in books from The Babysitters' Club or the Sweet Valley High series. These stories were about middle-class preteens who dutifully did their chores, loved and obeyed their parents, and cared about the children for whom they baby-sat.

The girls read these books in an unexpected way, however. The girls identified with the female characters because those characters helped them to feel more competent and confident. The characters were not seen just as baby-sitters but as people doing something praiseworthy, challenging, and worthwhile that gave them agency or an effectual way of acting on the world. The girls thought of the series' characters as earning money or manipulating actions for their own purposes, acting as agents in their own right. Girls seemed to admire female characters' risk-taking behaviors. One girl said of a character, "I love it when she gets into trouble. Those are the books I like" (Cherland & Edelsky, 1993, p. 35).

The New Town girls demonstrated their desire for agency as they read assigned readings, as well as books of their own choosing. For example, after one girl read *The Secret Garden* (Burnett, 1987), she commented that she did not like the boy's (Colin's) bossing of the girl, Mary. She remarked, "If I was Mary, I'd just tell him to stop it" (p. 33). When the teacher asked that students think of a gift they would give characters in the novel, *The Book of Three* (Alexander, 1999), the girls decided that the female character, Eilonwy, should receive a sword because, "She always wanted to fight and everything. She didn't want to be considered just a little girl" (p. 33). The New Town girls valued stories that showed possibilities for agency and "resisted or renegotiated the cultural messages that conveyed images of female passivity and submissiveness" (p. 36).

The girls' desire for agency was evident in their daily lives and in their recommendations of books to each other. Books like *Julie of the Wolves* (Craighead, 1972) and *Kid Power* (Pfeffer, 1977) were enthusiastically reviewed because the female characters were smart and independent. In their daily lives, the girls resisted adults' allocation of their time and, instead, read their series books in class or at home rather than doing schoolwork or chores.

Although the girls read for agency, cultural constraints appeared to counter and silence their aspirations. For example, the girls were exposed to the horror genre in forms like movies, music, videos, television, and books. They read a range of scary stories along a continuum from Nancy Drew mysteries, which they perceived they had outgrown, to Stephen King novels. A potent theme in this genre is that of sexual aggressor and victim, stories of female characters who are victimized and powerless. Cherland and Edelsky (1993) stated,

> The girls were learning to enjoy horror. They were being encouraged and encouraging each other to move along a continuum of horror stories that began with female characters who could understand and control what threatened them, and ended with victims who were horribly abused and finally obliterated. (p. 41)

Reading horror stories worked against the girls' desire for agency because they were receiving the message that "girls are not free agents. Moving in the world is dangerous. There are forces out there that will get you if you don't watch out" (p. 42). Hence, Cherland and Edelsky asserted that the culture had countered resistance with the publication of horror stories.

Like Cherland and Edelsky, Christian-Smith (1993a) examined resistance in her study of 29 junior high school girls in the midwestern United States. The girls in the focal group were considered reluctant readers by their teachers, but they were actually habitual readers of romance fiction. Their reading of romance fiction had strong oppositional tones, and the romance fiction stories were read to infuse energy, interest, and meaning into their reading classes and to help the girls acquire some power and control over one part of their education. In doing so, the girls decentered the teacher's traditional authority regarding choice of reading material. The girls' actions embodied the assertiveness of the girls they read about, and they challenged their teachers' power to determine the best texts for them.

However, the girls' opposition to authorized texts of instruction worked against them academically. The girls' lack of knowledge from reading those texts, combined with their teachers' rejection of romance novels as acceptable reading and a lack of communication between the girls and their teachers, created the risk of not graduating from high school or qualifying for only low-skill exploitative jobs. Their romance reading prepared them for entering society only as middle- and working-class women. The findings regarding lack of trust in relationships between teachers and students were supported by Carol Leroy's (1995) study of inner-city fifth-grade girls' opposition to their teachers whom they did not trust and in-school reading.

Discussion

Each of these studies illustrated one of four themes: (1) the importance of text and method in literature response; (2) gendered reading preferences and practices; (3) oppression or constraint of instructional and social context; and (4) opposition, accommodation, and resistance in reading. The first of these themes, the importance of text and method in reader response, addressed the conditions that make peer-led discussions successful. When reader response is interpreted as students putting themselves in the place of a character and relating their own experiences to those of the character, students' tendencies are to bring their stereotypical understandings of gender to their readings. Children also have a tendency to think in terms of boys' books and girls' books and respond accordingly. These works of fiction can be an enculturating mechanism by which males and females learn or reinforce their traditional gender roles.

To counteract these tendencies, it is important that students be exposed to books that portray both females and males in nontraditional roles. Also, the typical lack of structure in literature-response groups allows students to speak to each other in ways informed by their gendered beliefs in both their language patterns and their interpretations. When teachers become active participants in these groups and present and discuss alternative models of gender representation, students can be helped to deconstruct their gendered understandings.

The second theme, gendered reading preferences and practices, illustrated how ingrained students' understandings of gender constrain and are reinforced by their texts of choice. Researchers noted a multiplicity of ways in which gender, as a social construction, influenced students' choices and responses to literature. Most students preferred to read books about characters of their own sex in which males were adventurers and females nurturers of relationships. Boys tended to prefer nonfiction (aside from male-oriented, superhero comic books) and did not relate well to in-school reading in which most literature consisted of the fiction preferred by females. Teenage girls preferred to read romance novels or teen magazines, which was a form of reading not presented or valued in schools.

These discrepancies between students' in-school reading requirements and their out-of-school reading preferences may cause both males and females to enjoy and relate to their out-of-school reading more than their in-school reading. These unsanctioned texts can have powerful impacts on their readers. For example, girls' reading of teen romance novels and magazines can teach them values of consumerism, guide their behavior in interacting with boys, and reinforce their social-class positions; young males reading comics may find models of moral behavior while absorbing society's notions of masculinity as powerful, tough, successful, and independent.

These studies show the importance of bridging the gap between students' out-of-school reading and their in-school reading. Perhaps, if teachers were to allow students' reading choices like these into the classroom as Osmont (1987) did and teach students how to deconstruct them, students' selections and interpretations of texts might be less gendered. Making students aware that they can be positioned by the texts that they read will help them to develop as critical readers, will expand their notions of what counts as reading, and will help them to read strategically.

The third theme, oppression or constraint of instructional and social context, was illustrated by the studies that identified how teachers, parents, peers, and cultural norms can constrain literacy development. Teachers' instructional practices of selecting books for boys from a district-approved list and following reading with journals, tests, and weekly grades resulted in boys' beliefs that reading was work and that reading fiction was a school task. Teachers did not count boys' own use of their preferred texts. Teachers can constrain female students' interpretations of texts by never allowing them to read from a critical perspective. Parents may also constrain literacy development by encouraging boys in sports and, therefore, discouraging the enjoyment of and time available for reading. Adolescent boys may constrain each other by their beliefs that being popular is best achieved by competing with others in sports, not through academic achievement or reading. Family members can also constrain literacy development with their gendered cultural expectations, such as believing that a woman's place is in the home and, therefore, not supporting females' efforts to read and write.

These social and cultural constraints demonstrate how much learners have to overcome to become literate. The studies raise awareness of the school and home conditions that contribute to gendered literacy practices. Again, these studies make a case for allowing students to read materials of their choice in school and to help students learn to read these materials with a critical perspective. Teachers can use gendered texts to model how to resist the authority and values embedded in them. By doing so, students can learn how to read against text and to critically question the values those texts relate.

The fourth theme, opposition, accommodation, and resistance in reading, was illustrated in studies in which females and males negotiated meaning as they engaged with a text's depiction of gendered expectations and behaviors and as they drew on their own experiences and perceptions. These studies show how readers may accommodate by conforming to the gender roles represented in a text or may resist a text by questioning those roles and arriving at their own interpretations. Students may also demonstrate their desire for agency through their selections of texts.

In these studies, researchers noted a multiplicity of ways in which gender as a social construction influenced students' choices and responses to literature. Almost all the studies focused on classroom practice and ramifications, and nearly all briefly addressed the cultural and political contexts of texts and reading. Davies (1993) addressed the latter issue at length and proposed that political changes, as well as changes in interactions, must take place if we are to be rid of male-female dualism. As Davies (1989) suggested, gendered behaviors and attitudes are so embedded in approved dominant discourses that their creation and maintenance are invisible and also intractable. Children need to be helped to see gendered attitudes and behaviors and to realize how they can be altered. By doing so, teachers can create a pedagogy that situates reading not only as a social act, but a political one as well (Finders, 1999).

Recommendations for Instruction

These studies offered both direct and implicit suggestions for instructional practice. First, texts should be examined to determine their messages about gender. Children's books are an enculturating mechanism through which students learn traditional gender roles—girls learn to be nurturers and boys learn to be adventurers (Nauman, 1997). Therefore, it is important to produce and to use excellent examples of children's literature that do not replicate these stereotypical views of gender and that present alternative gender roles. Doing so can move readers beyond dichotomous thinking toward multiple ways of knowing and being (Johnson & Fox, in press).

Second, reading materials in the classroom should be expanded beyond the typical and traditional literature. Several studies gave evidence of the benefits of allowing nontraditional forms of literature into the classroom and expanding notions of what counts as reading. Allowing students the freedom to read comic books, magazines, newspapers, manuals, or web pages in class can also help instill the notion that reading is enjoyable, and thereby may serve to expand students' reading interests. In addition, Christian-Smith (1993a, 1993b) advocated that more expository or informational texts be included in classroom choices because they are the discourses of power. Knowledge gained from expository text in trade books and multiple texts is academically important and can help students graduate, get jobs, and gain access to the dominant power structure.

Third, students should be taught to read against text. Teachers can do so with texts that are included both in the classroom and self-selected by students outside the classroom. With modeling from the teacher and classroom discussions that focus on multiple ways of being, students can be asked to rewrite stereotypical stories and provide their own character portrayals and events. In addition, rather than force students to hide their preferred texts, classrooms may become appropriate places to teach students to examine critically the gendered messages in popular press. Finders (1996) suggested that students be guided to compare critically the messages in different magazines such as *Sassy* and *Teen Voice*, which are alternative magazines with no advertisements. Teachers can help students do so by modeling critical questioning while reading. Students can learn to monitor the messages they absorb from their readings by asking questions such as, What is the mission statement of this magazine? To what gender, race, and class does this publication appeal? How do the ads and articles in this magazine make me feel?

Finally, teachers can incorporate literature-study groups. To address criticisms of unstructured reader-response groups (e.g., perpetuation of gender stereotypes by attempts to identify with the characters), Cherland (1992) advocated literature-study groups that required critical and collaborative study of a text and of an author's craft. Literature-study groups convey pedagogy that values equality. In students' close reading and repeated study of a text, they can begin to think critically about literature. In fiction, students should be supported in discovering ways of relating to characters that are unlike themselves. Doing so involves helping children to engage in critical readings of different types of texts through teacher modeling and discussions. Using texts that challenge the status quo may encourage awareness and understanding of multiple realities. Students should be taught to recognize contradictions between popular fiction's version of social relations and their own lives. In reading and discussing informational text, students should be asked to provide evidence from the text that supports their opinions. Those who are less hesitant to read and discuss their reading will feel more confident and be more inclined to read with a rationale for their ideas.

Recommendations for Research

Future research should acknowledge the influence of multiple subjectivities that interact with gender. Although some studies examined the complexities of issues like these and provided recommendations for interrupting gendered practice, many treated gender as a category and essentialized females and males. Middle- or upper middle-class white students were most often the focus of study. There were few analyses of participants' race or ethnicity. In many studies, either there was no mention of participants' ethnicity or socioeconomic status, or there was simply a brief description of the setting for the study. In addition, most authors did not include information about their own ethnicity, background, socioeconomic status, or their values and ideologies, nor did they reveal how they influenced or were influenced by the research. In these studies, there was little sense of the researchers' part in the study or description of how the experience of the study changed them or their points of view. The absence of author and participant information created little context for a study and, therefore, alluded to the essentialist notion that all males and females of all ages, socioeconomic statuses, races, and ethnicities are alike in their gendered interactions with texts.

Therefore, this literature demonstrates the need for expansion of data collection and analysis in research on gender and reading. These studies, through the paucity of attention to multiple subjectivities, demonstrate the need to focus on participants from socioeconomic classes other than the middle- or upper middle class, as well as those from diverse racial and ethnic groups. Until researchers are conscious of and explicit about their participants' multiple subjectivities, and until researchers consider those subjectivities in their analyses, the literature will remain rife with essentialist notions of the influence of gender on reading.

It also would be useful to continue a line of inquiry exploring teaching strategies that promote multiple perspectives and combat gendered responses to text. Of particular importance is continued research on ways to encourage and support reading against text and develop critical literacy strategies. In addition, more research should focus on literature-study groups, proposed by Cherland (1994) as an alternative to literature-response groups, to determine how these structures may help students resist gendered messages in texts.

CHAPTER 4

Studies on Gender and Writing

Characteristics of the Studies

Forty-two observational studies were conducted that examined gender differences in and through students' writing. Most of these studies were conducted in the United States (77%), with 10% conducted in Canada, 7% in the United Kingdom, 2% in Australia, 2% in the Caribbean, and 2% in Eastern Europe. The ethnicity of first authors was not stated and could not be inferred in 49% of the studies. The ethnicity of the researchers was stated in only 22% of the studies. For those studies in which ethnicity was stated or inferred, 39% were conducted by either European American or Caucasian women. Ninety-three percent of the first authors were female; 12% of first or second authors were listed as male. Most researchers conducted their investigations from several frameworks. The most common of these was some type of feminism, such as black, poststructural, liberal, nonspecified, and critical feminisms (71%), or literacy as a social practice (44%). Other frames included language as a social practice/sociolinguistics (34%), social constructivism (20%), and critical literacy (2%). The most common type of research was qualitative (29%), with 17% case studies and 15% teacher action research or a combination of methods.

Ninety-three percent of the studies included female participants. Studies tended to be conducted with either primary children or older students (32%), with 11% middle school or junior high students, 19% high school students, 26% adults, and only 11% intermediate-elementary students. Ethnicity of the students was not specified in 36% of the studies.

The studies included 39% white participants (i.e., European American, Canadian, and Australian); 17% of participants were of African descent, and 7% were Native American, Aboriginal (Australian), or Puerto Rican. Socioeconomic status of participants was not identified in 39% of the studies. Of the studies that did identify participants' socioeconomic status, 32% focused on middle class to upper middle class, 20% included lower class participants, and 7% of participants were living at or below poverty level.

Themes

Three themes resulted from our analyses across the studies of gender and writing:

1. writing as a gendered social practice

2. students writing gender differently on their own

3. writing gender within sites of possibilities

A few studies informed more than one of the identified themes. In most cases, we chose to discuss each study in relation to only one of the themes it informed. These themes are identified and exemplified in the following sections.

Writing as a Gendered Social Practice

Ten studies told stories of how writing as a social practice shaped and is shaped by gendered identities (Brown, 1997; Dyson, 1994, 1995, also reported in 1997; Finders, 1996; Laidlaw, 1998; Orellana, 1995; Phinney, 1994; Schultz, 1996; Waff, 1994; Wheeler, 1986; Widerberg, 1998). One social practice of particular interest is note writing. Note writing, an unofficial school literacy practice, shaped and was shaped by middle school girls' gendered identities. For instance, in Margaret Finders's (1996) study, note writing was seen as an unofficial school ritual used by girls to maintain social status and mark themselves as girls of a certain sort. Two groups of girls, the Queens and the Cookies, were the focus of this year-long ethnographic study. Each group established their own practices for note writing, such as private codes (e.g., N. M. H. meant not much here) and proper ways to fold their notes. Such practices identified the girls as belonging to either the Queens or the Cookies. Each social group shared similar social class and ethnic backgrounds. Note writing as a genre had its rules and rituals that were strictly enforced. For example, notes were to be passed only to friends of equal social status. If a girl did not know her place within the social hierarchy and wrote to a more popular girl, she became the object of ridicule.

Similarly, Vicki Brown (1997), in a study of four diverse schools, found that notes passed by sixth-grade boys and girls followed certain patterns that marked their membership in gendered social groups. She found gender differences in both the form and the content of the notes. For example, in an analysis of the content, Brown found that boys chose to draw (instead of write about) sport figures, boats, cars, and conflicts reconstructed from television or comic books. Conversely, girls wrote notes that Brown considered relational and friendly, with topics that included concerns about looks, relationships, and individuals. Mary Alice Wheeler (1985) observed similar findings in the content of notes written by the fifth-grade girls and boys of her study. Like Brown and Finders, Wheeler portrayed note writing as an important social practice for negotiating and constructing social networks and gendered identities.

Gendered identities also were constructed and maintained as young students wrote during free writing time at school. Often, these gendered identities were constructed along rigid stereotypical lines. The story of Jennifer, a fictionalized kindergarten student, was a particularly poignant example of this rigidity. Linda Laidlaw (1998) wrote Jennifer's story based on data collected in her kindergarten classroom. The story of Jennifer's writing experiences exemplified the power of social contexts to inform children's writings. Jennifer, a girl of mixed ethnicity in a suburban classroom of predominately white students, wrote about friendship, inclusion, acceptance, and her dreams but rarely shared her own experiences. As she became a member of a group of girls, her writing began to resemble that of the others in the group. Jennifer's stories reflected her quest for acceptance and her desire to be like the white middle-class girls in her class. Similarly, in a study by Anne Haas Dyson (1994), Sammy, a new African American student in an urban second-grade class, wrote to fit in with his peers. Dyson described how Sammy's writing helped him to gain status in the classroom as he wrote the expected male-hero-action stories about X-Men, which usually did not include girls. Sammy found a way, however, to successfully include girls without losing status with the boys by declaring that X-Men women were "as strong as men" (p. 228).

Another 11 qualitative studies demonstrated how writing as a gendered social practice informed author voice, topic, and genre selection. In these studies, students' writing tended to shape and maintain a dualistic perspective on gender (Brodkey, 1989; Burdick, 1997; Fleming, 1995; Hunt, 1995; Kamler, 1993, 1994, 1999; MacGillivray & Martinez, 1998; Maher, Wade, & Moore, 1997; Orellana, 1995; Scarboro, 1994; Simon, 1997). Within this perspective, boys and girls possessed oppositional qualities and characteristics, and these differences were reflected in their choice of author voice, topic, and genre. A dualistic perspective on gender is prevalent in society's expectations for children and defines boys as aggressive, strong, and powerful and girls as passive, weak, and needy. The strength of this perspective to inform student writing is evident even in the writing of very young children.

Laurie MacGillivray and Ana Martinez (1998) conducted a study that demonstrated this dualistic perspective. They examined primary-aged Latina/Latino, Asian American, and European American boys' and girls' story writing and found that during free-choice writing, males were portrayed in the stories as heroes and females as either victims or those in need. The lack of female heroes and the prominence of male heroes was characteristic of these young writers' stories and supported a dualistic thinking of gender. Likewise, in Susan Fleming's (1995) study, second-grade students wrote along stereotypical gender lines. The boys in her study tended to write adventure and sport stories, whereas the girls wrote stories about relationships and wrote descriptions of events. Similarly, Barbara Kamler (1994) described how two young Australian primary-school students—a boy and a girl— wrote about their experiences. Although both children wrote in the same genre of personal experience, the boy represented his experiences as acting on the world, whereas the girl portrayed her experiences in terms of her observations rather than her actions. In other words, she wrote a more flowery description of the event rather than writing about the action of the event. For example, the boy wrote, "We had sand fights," and the girl wrote, "I saw two white horses and a black horse" (p.169).

For older writers, topic selections also differed by gender. One example was found in Susan Hunt's (1995) study of bilingual high school students in Puerto Rico. After examining 196 free-choice writing samples, Hunt determined that males were more likely to write about philosophical questions, adventures, and social problems, whereas female students were more likely to write about relationships and subjects closer to home such as family and the classroom. In another study of high school writers, Tracey Burdick (1997) determined that topic selection for research papers also differed by gender. She noted that adolescent girls often selected female authors to research, whereas the boys never selected a female author to research.

Other studies we reviewed focused on the relationship between gender and audience. These studies point to the strong influence of audience—both teacher audience (Cleary, 1996; Fox, 1986; Haswell & Haswell, 1995; Peterson, 1998, 1999; Roen, 1992) and peer audience (Fiesta, 1997; Henkin, 1995; McAuliffe, 1993/1994; Meinhof, 1997), on the writers' use of gendered writing practices. For example, Shelly Peterson (1998), found that when teachers were the audience for sixth-grade student writers, gender affected evaluation. When students' writing did not conform to teachers' gendered expectations (e.g., a female student wrote a violent action story, or a male student wrote an emotional poem), the teacher judged the writing samples more critically in narrative evaluations. It appears that students would quickly learn and conform to teachers' gendered expectations in order for their writing to be judged more positively. This phenomenon also was evident in Linda Cleary's (1996) investigation of high school writers. Male and female students wrote what they thought the teacher expected. Interestingly, males were more apt than females to integrate what they wanted to write with teachers' expectations. Consequently, male students derived more personal satisfaction from writing than their female peers did.

Peer reaction to writing also contributed to how writers constructed gender in their writing. Roxanne Henkin (1995) observed first-grade students during writing workshop and determined that boys and girls seldom conferenced with one another. Boys said they did not conference with girls because they thought girls were not interested in and did not know anything about boys' topics. Girls did not conference with boys for fear the boys would laugh at them. In this first-grade classroom, the boys and girls limited their thinking about gender by strategically excluding voices that might challenge stereotypical gendered writing practices. Marjorie Orellana (1995) and Heather Blair (1996) reported similar findings in their observations of children creating their own gender-segregated writing groups. Sheila McAuliffe (1993/1994) found, however, that mixed-sex writing groups encouraged second graders to cross gender boundaries and use both stereotypical male and female story style characteristics in their story writing.

Students Writing Gender Differently on Their Own

Although we have described at length the strength of social contexts and dominant constructions of gender to influence students' writing in stereotypical ways, there were examples of individual students who dared to cross gender lines through their writing (Blair, 1996; Dyson, 1997; MacGillivray & Martinez, 1998; Moss, 1993; Orellana, 1995; Simmons, 1997). One particularly powerful example came from Tina, an African American girl in Dyson's (1995) 3-year study of the social and textual lives of primary-age students. Tina was the only third-grade girl to write superhero stories and to continually question the boys about how boys positioned girls as victims in their stories. Tina's critiques and resistant writings were supported by her teacher's interest in extending the students' ideas. For instance, the teacher supported Tina's critique in which she pointed out to the boys that there were female X-Men (popular superheroes) in the cartoons, but not in any of the boys' stories. The teacher's support encouraged students' explorations of gender representations in school writing.

Like Tina, Angelique, a 15-year-old black Jamaican girl living in London, England, explored alternative gendered practices in her writing (Moss, 1993). Throughout the school year, Angelique wrote romance stories in which girls rejected boys, and boys were not the focus of a female's unconditional love and emotion. Her stories did not end with the traditional happy ending. It seemed that Angelique changed the romance genre to better match the experiences of people in her social and cultural world. It is interesting to note that the narrator of her stories seemed to be white. Angelique explained that she had no black models to guide her writing of romance. All the romance books she had read featured white characters. She wrote stories that represented her complex and contradictory life as a black woman within a white culture. They also reflected her active challenging of accepted gendered norms.

In Laurie MacGillivray and Ana Martinez's (1998) analysis of 13 classroom-published stories in a mixed-aged, multiethnic, primary classroom revealed another romance story written with a not-so-happy ending. A female student, Rachel, wrote a story about a lonely princess who committed suicide because she did not have the clothes or the ticket for the ball. The story ended when the other princesses returned from the ball, found the lonely princess dead, and killed themselves. At first glance, this story seems to be a traditional, cross-gendered writing practice—a girl writing a violent tale without male characters. The researchers, however, suggested that Rachel's story, even without a visible male character, depicted male power and women as victims.

Two stories that did disrupt the views of women as victims and men as powerful were written by Elsa, one of Rachel's classmates. One of Elsa's stories did not differentiate the characters by sex. The other story had all female characters and did not portray females as victims or allude to men's dominance in any way. Elsa was a young girl whose parents encouraged her to think beyond stereotypes and be critical of mass media. Along with Tina and Angelique, Elsa represents the few students in the studies we reviewed who have the courage to write against the gender expectations.

Like Tina, Angelique, and Elsa, the eighth-grade, multiethnic, working-class girls (e.g., Ukrainian, Metis, Iraqi, Aboriginal, El Salvadorian, Mexican, and European American) in Heather Blair's (1996) studies crossed gender lines in their writing. Blair examined 80 finished pieces in 16 girls' writing folders. Topic and genre choice did not fit the patterns previously reported by researchers like Donald Graves (1975) and Hunt (1995). The topics the girls wrote about included danger, family, relationships, gangs, death, emotions, current events, adventure, horror, boyfriends, philosophy, love, family violence, and teen pregnancy. Blair believed the perceived freedom of the writing workshop encouraged the girls to reflect on their complex lives. Although this is a plausible explanation, these girls' writing, like Tina's, Elsa's, and Angelique's, reflected the contrast they saw between their working-class lives in western Canada and the images portrayed by the mass media and in texts and in their local interactions within a dominant white middle-class society. There was no evidence in their classroom of texts or discussions that would have helped them understand the cross-cultural contrasts they lived, and the girls rarely shared during author's chair (classroom time for students to share stories) for fear of the boys' negative responses. Writing became a private practice for these girls only to be shared with girlfriends if anyone at all. Even so, the girls explained that writing provided them opportunities to construct their ideas and understandings of their lives as girls.

Writing Gender Within Sites of Possibilities

Seven of the studies we reviewed examined the impact of sites of possibilities, which provide spaces for students to explore gender (Blake, 1997; Harper, 1998; Henry, 1998; Luce-Kapler, 1999; Norris-Handy, 1996; Osborn, 1991; Utley & Mathews, 1996). We describe four writing projects that we believe could be integrated into writing classrooms and offer insights into practices intended to create sites of possibilities for student writers.

The girls in a fifth-grade classroom in inner-city Chicago, Illinois, USA, were provided an all-girl space to share their writing (Blake, 1997). Like the girls in Blair's (1996) study, these girls from multiethnic backgrounds rarely shared their writing during the author's chair time in their classroom. When researcher Brett Elizabeth Blake observed this, she created a private place for the girls away from the boys. Meeting once or twice a week, Blake facilitated an all-girls writers' circle and exposed the girls to a variety of texts that represented different genres, topics, themes, and author voice. The girls began to challenge traditional notions of gender in and through their writing. For example, girls wrote about injustices they experienced as girls and experimented with writing about violence. They also began sharing their writings with each other.

Blake surmised that the writing circle became a site for the girls to write and speak about their complex and contradictory lives as poor urban girls.

Rebecca Luce-Kapler (1999) also facilitated all-female writing groups (e.g., a group of English teachers, a group of adult women, and a group of adolescent girls) to open up the possibilities of an evolving female self. For the purpose of this review, we focused on the after-school adolescent writing group that was facilitated by Luce-Kapler and Sidonie, an English teacher. The teenage girls were from predominantly white, middle-class families in suburban Canada. The facilitators gradually gained the trust and respect of the girls by listening, sharing, and writing alongside the girls. They also never required the girls to share their writing and spent several meetings doing fun writing practices that were not too challenging or threatening (Luce-Kapler, personal e-mail communication, November 11, 1999). For example, the girls brought in favorite songs and responded to the songs by flow writing (nonstop, timed writing) or wrote about objects or pictures. One such activity had the girls choose a button and write about the memories it stirred. As trust and comfort was developed, the facilitators exposed the girls to literature intended to inspire them to move beyond their comfort levels and to expose them to different literary forms. For example, they read "The Semiotics of Sex" by Jeanette Winterson (1995) and poetry by Lorna Crozier (Luce-Kapler, personal e-mail communication, November 11, 1999). The girls in the writing group also learned to sense how words position them in gendered ways through discourse analysis. For example, the girls listed the nouns, verbs, and important phrases used in one of their writing pieces and then sorted them into three categories: wishes and dreams, actions, and feelings (Luce-Kapler, personal e-mail communication, November 11, 1999).

The girls also experimented by rewriting several pieces using different genres. They began to move away from the real-life narrative style to fictionalized representations of their lives. Writing became a subjunctive way for the girls to challenge and explore the possibilities in their lives. Overall, the girls described their experiences in the writing group as wonderful. The author reported that after the project ended, some of the girls continued to meet in their own writing groups and explore their identities through writing.

Unlike the girls in Luce-Kapler's writing group, the girls in Helen Harper's (1995) feminist avant-garde writing group were not so positive about their experiences. The project, in a suburban Toronto, Canada, school, was intended to offer girls an opportunity to read and write differently. Six 17-year-old Canadian girls (four Caucasian and two Asian) attended the group as an option in their creative writing class. They met once or twice a week during class time. The students read, discussed, and wrote responses to a selection of feminist literature chosen by the researcher. The literature included works by contemporary Canadian feminist avant-garde writers. All the writing selected for the project offered a wide range of unconventional uses of language, theme, and literary form.

Discussion of the text often focused on questions of how women were represented in text, how sexual differences and relations are understood, and how gender relations operated in real life. Although the girls actively participated in discussions about the literature and extended their discussion in response journals and creative writing pieces, it was apparent to the researcher that reading and writing differently was difficult and not desirable for the girls. The girls found it particularly unpalatable to read against heterosexual relations. For example, one of the girls, Rebecca, had to rethink what writing meant to her. Rebecca insisted that creative writing was a hobby and a way to explore her heterosexual identity and personal feelings. This belief fueled her resistance to feminist writing. Despite her resistance, Rebecca's exposure to feminist literature and her experiences within the feminist writing group opened avenues for her to explore gendered social identities and inequities in and through writing. Like the other girls in the project, Rebecca began to explore oppression in her writing.

Our final example of a feminist writing project is Susan Osborn's (1991) writing pedagogy used in a college feminist writing class. Unlike the writing projects described previously, this writing class was attended by men and women, and it was not a required course. Osborn based her pedagogy on Adrienne Rich's (1979) notion of re-vision and Florence Howe's (1984) model of re-vision, which is recursive rather than mechanistic. Rich explains re-vision as a look back or seeing old texts with fresh eyes. Howe's model of re-vision recognizes and respects ambiguities, continuities, and recursive thinking. Both of these processes require an examination of old text, and a repositioning of self in relation to others. Osborn taught re-vision/revision as a skill and a concept to the students and provided opportunities to practice these skills. In addition to teaching about re-vision/revision, Osborn guided the students through reading feminist literature—essays, plays, and fiction. The students answered study questions that encouraged an understanding of how language constructs gender. For example, one question asked the students to list the violent, abusive, and degrading words used to describe women, male and female body parts, or sexual intercourse in a Norman Mailer story, "The Time of Her Time." The next question asked them to list verbs used to describe heterosexual intercourse from a revised female-centered perspective (e.g., encircle, surround, engulf, make love). The students compared their words to Mailer's words.

Students also participated in a variety of writing assignments that included individual and group re-vision and revision. For example, one writing assignment required small groups of students to discuss and then write individually about a time that they were silenced, and to report on what those silences indicated about the relationship between gender and language. Another assignment asked students to consider how the language used to represent body parts indicated a relationship between language and gender. A third assignment asked small groups of students to note patterns in their final papers that indicated a relationship between gender and language. For instance, one group explored why women tended to use more slashes in their papers than men did.

Discussion

Three themes were discussed in this section: (1) writing as a gendered social practice, (2) students writing gender differently on their own, and (3) writing gender within sites of possibilities. The first theme, writing as a gendered social practice, pointed to the power of the social contexts—how peers, teachers, and society-at-large influence student writings. The studies demonstrated how writing as a social practice shapes and is shaped by gender. Students participating in these studies wrote to fit in with particular gendered groups and learned to do gender appropriately as they wrote and shared their writings in schools. Many of the studies in this theme ignored the political nature of writing, and instead, opted by default to present a more dualistic view of gendered writing practices. For example, researchers presented evidence that male and female students wrote differently and described how gender affected the evaluation of students' writing. They did not, however, discuss the politics behind these differences or present the teachers' or students' values, beliefs, and ideologies that shaped the writing instruction and writing practices. Investigators also did not examine how teachers' interactions with students may have privileged certain writing practices over others. Nor did the researchers reflect on how their own values, beliefs, and ideologies may have influenced their interpretations of their data. For example, only 21% of the researchers stated their ethnicity. This sort of information about researchers (and participants) is important in understanding and interpreting research (see Stanley & Wise, 1993).

The second theme, students writing gender differently on their own, described how a few students went against gender stereotypes to explore and construct different versions of gender. Even though the peers of these students conformed to traditional gender practices and representations, they did not. Common to all these students was their minority status within dominant white middle-class society. These students' writings, in particular, hint at how gender interacts with ethnicity and social class to produce different views of gender. Perhaps the status and experiences of the minority girls made it easier for them to write against traditional gender stereotypes.

This theme provided us with more questions than answers and made us wonder about allowing students the freedom to choose writing topics, genres, and author voice. Are students really free to make these decisions, or does the influence of peers, teachers, and society-at-large inhibit their so-called freedom? We also wondered if more students would have written gender differently if their teachers had facilitated talk about gender representation in texts or had exposed them to books and other texts that portrayed gender in a variety of nonstereotypical ways. Most importantly, we wondered what gave these girls the strength to write against gendered stereotypes.

The last theme, writing gender within sites of possibilities, explored feminist writing projects that provided students with opportunities to explore and disrupt traditional gender stereotypes in and through writing. Unlike the students who wrote against gender stereotypes on their own, these students were asked to participate in specific conscious-raising activities that were designed to develop an awareness of the relationship between language and gender. We believe that it is necessary for teachers and researchers to reflect on what students are learning about gender as they write and what writing does to them as gendered individuals. It is time to move beyond the acknowledgment that differences exist between male's and female's writing and start developing ways to disable dominant ideologies of gender, race, and class that keep dominant systems of power in place in and through writing. We suggest that literacy researchers acknowledge the political nature of writing and bravely forge ahead, as the researchers we have highlighted within the last theme have done.

We are reminded of Barbara Kamler's (1999) explanation that writing instruction is political in terms of the wider social and political contexts that shape the work of teachers of writing and stated, "the values, beliefs, and ideologies of 'New Times' are not just a backdrop to our teaching" (p. 2). In other words, the beliefs, values, and ideologies of writing teachers shape how they teach and evaluate writing and how learners come to know what counts as good writing. Writing is also political in that it is a social practice, and its uses and functions are never neutral; that is, meanings that are constructed in and through writing tend to produce and maintain dominant systems of power that are seldom equal (Comber & Kamler, 1997, in Kamler, 1999). For example, systems of power were working when the first-grade girls and boys in Roxanne Henkin's (1995) study refused to peer conference with one another. The boys did not think that girls could understand what they were writing about, and the girls were afraid the boys would laugh at them. These are the kinds of risks that students take when sharing their writing with each other.

Recommendations for Instruction

We offer four suggestions derived from the research on gender and writing for those interested in creating sites of possibilities for students as writers. First, a safe and conducive writing environment needs to be created in which students and teachers are encouraged to experiment with different writing practices. In most of the cases we reviewed, this meant all-girl writing groups. In one case, it meant a college feminist writing classroom. Common to each case was the trust and respect that students built with one another and with the teacher.

Second, a variety of different kinds of texts and literature needs to be available for students to read and examine. Participants in the writing projects were exposed to a wide range of genres, such as poetry, essays, plays, and fiction. Many of these texts portrayed the characters in nonstereotypical ways, presented unconventional themes, and used language in nontraditional ways. Careful selection of literature is crucial. As Pam Gilbert (1983) recommended, writing that explores women's feelings, experiences, and needs should be brought into the classroom as models for girls' own writing, and literature with alternative portrayals of gender roles should be brought into the classroom as well. Perhaps the students in Helen Harper's (1998) study would not have resisted feminist, lesbian avant-garde literature had they been gradually led to it.

Third, students need to be taught discourse analysis techniques. Discourse analysis provides students with tools to help them examine the relationship between language and gender. In the studies we reviewed, the results of a close analysis of words and phrases surprised the participants and contributed to their awareness of how gender was represented in texts.

Fourth, and perhaps the most powerful practice exhibited in the studies, was the experimentation by students with writing in different literary forms. This practice encouraged students to think differently about their gendered identities. We saw this as an especially important component in Osborn's feminist writing pedagogy and Luce-Kapler's writing group. Like Luce-Kapler, we believe that

> [P]erhaps the strongest [practice] was using different forms of writing to explore and interpret identity. By asking them to interpret and then rein-

terpret through narrative, poetry, plays, and discourse analysis, they could see how interpretations could be broadened, shifted, and changed. (Luce-Kapler, personal e-mail communication, November 11, 1999)

Recommendations for Research

Like Comber and Kamler (1997, in Kamler, 1999), we think it is important for teachers and researchers to reflect on what it is students are learning about gender as they write. We also need to explore what writing does to students' gendered identities. With this in mind, we offer the following suggestions for further research.

First, we believe it is time to move beyond researching the differences that exist between males' and females' writing. Rather, it is time to explore how social contexts and dominant ideologies keep these differences in place. We suggest that qualitative researchers acknowledge the political nature of writing and forge ahead by following the lead of researchers like Luce-Kapler (1999) and Harper (1995), who attempted to change gendered writing practices.

Second, we recommend that more research be conducted to examine how students' and teachers' formal and informal interactions favor certain writing practices over others. More studies need to be conducted, such as Peterson's (1998) investigation, to show how teachers' gender beliefs and expectations and the comments they make to students about their writing influence students' writing. Likewise, more studies like Finders (1996) are needed to explore how students' interactions regulate gendered writing practices.

Third, we need research to help us understand why some students write independently against gendered stereotypes. What is it about certain classroom or home environments that encourages or allows students to write against gender stereotypes? These questions seem worth pursuing, as research by Judith Solsken (1993) determined that structuring processes in the family and the classroom related to gender affected literacy learning. Studies like the ones conducted by Gemma Moss (1995) and Heather Blair (1996) intrigued us and made us want to know more about why minority girls tended to disrupt dualistic gender writing practices.

Finally, we believe more research needs to focus on the process of changing writing practices in school. We need to know more about what happens when students and teachers engage in activities such as discourse analysis, and students begin to become aware of how gender is represented in texts. Investigations like these should enable us to provide more insights into instructional practices that would enable students to become writers unconstrained by gendered ideas and environments.

CHAPTER 5

Studies on Gender and Electronic Text

Characteristics of the Studies

Six observational studies were located of gender and electronic or posttypographical text. Most were conducted in the United States (83%), although 17% were done in the United Kingdom. Five of the six studies were conducted from multiple frameworks, with 50% feminist frames, and 50% framed by a view of literacy as a social practice. Only one study stated both the ethnicity and gender of the author. Female researchers conducted 83% of the studies, and 67% were published studies.

Fifty percent of the studies included European American participants, 17% included African Americans, and 17% included Hispanics. Ethnicity of the informants was not stated in 33% of the studies. No studies were conducted exclusively of males' electronic interactions with males, but 17% were of only females' interactions. Most of the studies (67%) included both males and females, with 60% of elementary school age, 17% of middle school age, and 33% a combination of these or other ages such as college and high school students. Approximately 33% of the studies investigated working-class students and 33% investigated middle- to upper-class students.

Themes

Two themes resulted from our analyses of these studies:

1. using electronic text as a means to negotiate and enhance social relationships

2. disparate findings in gender equity through talking, reading, and writing with electronic text

These themes are identified and exemplified in the following sections.

Using Electronic Text as a Means to Negotiate and Enhance Social Relationships

Two studies demonstrated how females used electronic text to build and enhance their social relationships (Christie, 1995; Lewis & Fabos, 1999). In the first study, Alice Christie (1995) conducted a feminist research project in which she invited third, fourth, and fifth graders to a university campus for a series of computer information (i.e., e-mail and Internet search engines) and exploration sessions. The researcher let the students decide how to spend their time each day. Her goal was to understand how children viewed computers and telecommunications. She examined how she (as the teacher researcher) and the children supported or rejected gendered stereotypes during their interactions with computers and computer text. In doing so, Christie analyzed 750 pages of e-mail messages, including students' logs and newsletters, as well as her observations of and interviews with students.

Analysis of these data revealed that both girls and boys used computers to confirm gender stereotypes. The most common reason girls used computer text was for building relationships and communicating with others using fun technology. Twice as many girls than boys viewed computer text as a medium for connecting with others. Girls defined computers as tools that foster collaboration, connection, and communication. They used electronic text to share feelings, build friendships, and show care for others. Girls' writing topics centered on people.

Boys also used computer text in gendered ways. For example, boys used technology to search for and share factual information. They also used computer text to insult, tease, and test limits. Boys' writing topics centered on events and things such as computers and games.

Instances also were reported of both girls and boys using computers to defy gender stereotypes. These cases revealed nonstereotypical ways that boys and girls used computers and what topics they chose to write about online. For example, girls found computers fun for building independence and enhancing personal productivity, whereas boys also found, like girls did, that computers can be frustrating. Both boys and girls saw computers as tools for building relationships. Girls wrote about computers, learning, and research and wrote twice as many e-mail messages to the teacher researcher than did boys. Boys wrote about social concerns and family issues. Boys used technology to build friendships. Girls used technology to facilitate their knowledge of computers and telecommunications. Therefore, both boys and girls used computer text as a social medium for confirming and defying gender stereotypes.

Although some advances were made in defying gender stereotypes, Christie, like Alvermann and her colleagues (1997), concluded that gender bias is more unapparent and difficult to eliminate than expected. Christie also commented on her own gendered behavior, and noted that she treated boys and girls differently by interacting more and in different ways with boys than with girls, and by holding different expectations for boys than for girls. Although she considered a feminist perspective essential in interrupting gendered practice, she found that stance insufficient for eliminating culturally embedded gender biases.

The second study, conducted by Cynthia Lewis and Bettina Fabos (1999), focused on females' use of instant messaging (IM), which was created for brief, casual, real-time electronic communication. The researchers investigated IM by two European American females who were from working- and middle-class families and who were enrolled in a private middle school. The buddy list allows the IM user to know which e-mail-equipped friends or family members are online at a given time, and the user immediately can begin messaging with any of them. IM communications mimic face-to-face discussions; the norm is to send short, overlapping messages that can be continuously interrupted. Lewis and Fabos interviewed two girls (Sam and Karrie, who were friends) and collected videotaped sessions of the girls' IM to discover the IM's purpose in the girls' lives.

Lewis and Fabos found that the girls chatted online to negotiate and enhance their social relationships and social standing at school, while also establishing a social currency that kept them informed. Sam used IM to bond with Karrie and to gain some control in her social relationships. Sam and Karrie both reported that online conversations allowed for more ease and less awkwardness in communicating, particularly when talking to members of the opposite sex. IM also encouraged self-revelations not evident in telephone calls and face-to-face interactions.

For example, IM allowed boys to tell Sam and Karrie more than they normally would.

Lewis and Fabos (1999) noted that IM provided Sam and Karrie with "more space for play, parody, and performance" (p. 12) than oral discussions. They were able to manipulate their voice, tone, and subject matter to hide or transform their identities and to monitor the interactions of others. For example, when Sam and Karrie chose to enter chat rooms, they lied about their ages to pursue conversations with older people, controlling the rhetorical contexts of their interactions through careful consideration of issues related to status, age, and gender. In addition, Sam revealed how she manipulated online technology for purposes related to power and identity. She often turned off her buddy list indicator so friends could not tell when she was online and used IM to ask friends who was online at that time, who were they talking to, and what were they discussing. Karrie tracked her boyfriend into a chat room, assumed an online male identity of "Snowboarder 911" and attempted to find out what kind of conversations he was having. Karrie also investigated and tracked online "Junclily 24," a girl who mistakenly thought of Sam as her best IM buddy. Therefore, computer texts helped these girls learn reading and writing as social strategies. Sam and Karrie critically analyzed language in terms of the social context within which it was framed and in terms of what the texts could do for them. Lewis and Fabos concluded that online discussions may be more gender equitable than oral discussions.

Disparate Findings in Gender Equity Through Talking, Reading, and Writing With Electronic Text

In addition to the study by Lewis and Fabos (1999), four studies explored the question of gender equity through electronic discussions (Fey, 1997, 1998; Nicholson, Gelpi, Young, & Sulzby 1998; Pryor, 1995). Julie Nicholson, Adrienne Gelpi, Shannon Young, and Elizabeth Sulzby (1998) observed 36 first-grade students over 6 months to examine the relationship between gender and computer software usage. The study's goal was to describe the experiences of primary children working together to compose a story on computers with same-sex and opposite-sex peers by using an open-ended computer software program, Kid Pix. The researchers found gendered interactions in using the software program in dyads or small groups. Data showed that boys created competition by comparing stories and by pointing out differences in a competitive manner. For example, David critiqued and criticized the work of his partner Maria, but Maria did not do so with David's work. In other mixed-sex pairs, males destroyed female partners' confidence with constant critical remarks, threats, strong directives, and critiques. For example, Tyler criticized his partner Beth to the extent that he directed her to erase any trace of her contributions from the screen by using the Kid Pix eraser tools. Tyler also composed rules and limitations for Beth's behavior that placed her in a submissive position. For example, he informed her that she was not allowed to use the color green.

Conversely, females in mixed-sex pairs engaged in greater amounts of work to keep the pair on task, and sought to keep males' attention through direct requests and pleas. For example, Maria sought David's attention by calling his name, requesting his whereabouts, and pleading with him to return to the computer. Females in same-sex pairs set collaborative rules for taking turns at writing and remained focused on their own work except when interrupted by males. Females responded to each other's requests for information with collaborative and task-focused interactions. Their communications and their writings were inclusive and noncombative. Girls supported, encouraged, and collaborated with one another through noncompetitive and repeated turn taking.

John Pryor (1995) conducted a study in the United Kingdom with contrary results. Pryor examined the online interactions of male and female students in intermediate elementary school. The researcher observed dyads to identify the gender issues that emerged when students worked with electronic text.

The study was conducted in two phases. In the first phase, Pryor found that boys' domination of electronic text coincided with their ability. In order of dominance, boys who were most able were identified as most dominant, then less able boys, able girls, and finally, less able girls. More able boys marginalized less able girls. Surprisingly, only two of the four all-girl pairs allowed both partners equal access, and only one female pair worked collaboratively.

In the second phase, the female teacher conducted four interventions with her 9- and 10-year-old students to encourage partner focus, especially with the boys. First, the teacher explained to the students that the goal of good collaboration was as important as achieving any end product. She then spelled out how and when individual members of the group might be consulted and provided periodic and continual reminders to leave no one out of the group work. A second intervention was to give more praise to students on their group-work skills than on their end product. The third intervention was to raise group-work issues through group training exercises. One such exercise was Cooperative Squares (Kingston Friends Workshop Group, 1985) in which individuals through collaboration must arrange shapes to complete a square. The fourth intervention consisted of frequent discussions with the whole class about group issues, questionnaires to obtain students' comments on each computer session, and students' structured observations of each other. Although boys found it particularly difficult to focus on their partners at the beginning of the year, there was a general shift during the year to more partner-focused efforts.

Two studies conducted by Marion Fey (1997, 1998) also had disparate results for gender equity through communication with electronic texts. In her most recent study, Fey (1998) aimed to understand how a discussion of gender issues through electronic networking might affect the development of voice in 6 college women, from a feminist group, who organized and participated in online discussions with 7 male and 10 female students from an urban and a suburban high school. She also wanted to explore the ways in which electronic discussions facilitated the practice of critical literacy. Fey cited Lankshear and McLaren (1993) who defined critical literacy as using print skills to help subordinate groups engage in action aimed at challenging existing structures of inequality and oppression. In Fey's study, a focus on critical literacy reflected on power issues that focused on gender as experienced and understood by participants in the high school-college collaboration. The primary sources of data were transcripts of all messages sent to the computer discussion list. Other data included questionnaires and notes from open-ended interviews with members of the feminist group, as well as with three secondary students who participated heavily and relevantly in the electronic discussions.

Analyses of these data showed that electronic discussions provided an effective environment for the practice of critical literacy, as students named experiences relating to gender issues that touched their personal and professional lives. The freedom of computer networking provided the feminist group the freedom of time—time to think, reflect, write, and reread messages—enabling them to reflect on gendered circumstances in their own lives, as well as in the lives of others, and reinforce their commitment to feminism. As facilitators, these women also enabled secondary students to reflect on their own gendered circumstances. Electronic discussions provided an enabling environment for the development of voice in the presence of conflict. For example, a male senior from an urban high school, who called himself "Big Guy," denounced the merits of feminism. Big Guy's patriarchal language (condescending to females) invited controversy. The feminists disregarded differences in age, gender, race, and class by responding to this conflict and citing specific contributions of women that the patriarchal system had overlooked. In ways like these, students felt free to share their ideas and to disclose personal experiences that otherwise might not have been heard in oral discussions in classrooms.

Fey's earlier study (1997), however, had opposite results. In this investigation, Fey connected two preservice, secondary-education classrooms through computer-mediated discussions with students from two secondary schools. These discussions focused on ethics rather than gender issues. The researcher explored the consequences of computer-mediated communication for young women. Fey asked how reading and writing through computer text might afford a safe space for young women's development. In doing so, Fey collected transcripts of computer messages that she sent to her own preservice students and messages between participants and from computer consultants and school sponsors, questionnaires completed at the end of the computer discussion, notes from interviews with the high school students, and field notes.

Examination of these data showed that males assumed expert roles in discussions of topics like the death penalty and, particularly sports and the ethics involved with professional athletes' high salaries. Males' contributions outnumbered women's contributions 2 to 1. In doing so, males were able to establish power and independence through a sense of status and expertise. Males used sexist language and linear, hierarchical, and objective discourse to argue their views. Women's discourse typified exploratory and relational traits noted by sociolinguists like Lakoff (1975) and Gilligan (1982). Women in the study used personal experiences as connective language to support their positions. Their online messages worked toward building community and was characterized by respectful language in their disagreements.

Although many women's voices were heard clearly, there was still a mood of discouragement that left some young women marginalized by absence of voice. Fey found that the large number of participants created an unwieldy number of messages that the college students found too time-consuming to read in entirety. Masculine discourse seemed exaggerated throughout the study, particularly by the over-participation of one articulate male in high school, which contributed to the atmosphere of discouragement for young women. The antagonistic language of some males (whether combative, defensive, or sarcastic) inhibited the expression of voice among female participants. Fey (1997) noted that one female secondary student wrote,

> I don't know how to put it tactfully, so I'll be blunt. I did not enjoy participating in the discussion. As a result, I was an active reader, but an infrequent responder. I was intimidated by the personal attacks. I was hesitant to write my opinion. (p. 514)

Fey concluded that the impact of written speech and the freedom of computer-mediated discussion might play a role in the polarization of language styles.

Discussion

Two themes resulted from our analysis: (1) using electronic text as a means to negotiate and enhance social relationships, and (2) disparate findings in gender equity through talking, reading, and writing with electronic text. The first theme, using electronic text to negotiate and enhance social relationships, revealed ways in which both females and males used computer text to confirm gender stereotypes. In the studies that illustrated this theme, girls used electronic text to build relationships and connect with others, particularly by talking online, whereas boys tended to use computers to search for and share factual information, and their online communication intended to insult, tease, and test limits. Girls wrote stories that centered on people; conversely, boys' stories centered on events and things. Although instances were reported of individuals deviating from these patterns, students typically used computer communications in gendered ways.

The second theme, disparate findings in gender equity through talking, reading, and writing with electronic text, was discovered in studies that explored students' learning with computer text. Some studies showed that electronic text could help to make discussions more gender fair. This result, however, seems to have occurred only under one of two conditions: when students were discussing feminist issues or when students' genders were concealed with pseudonyms. In a similar way, studies of students' online writing were characterized by gendered interactions. Males created competition by critically comparing their stories with females' stories. Boys who had more ability with computers dominated access to writing with computers. Although some gender-fair nuances have been described, the qualitative research does not present a convincing case that talking, reading, or writing through electronic texts produces more gender equitable opportunities than other forms of communication in classrooms.

Recommendations for Instruction

Due to the small number of studies and the conflicting findings, we offer few recommendations for instruction. Interventions with electronic text are recommended, such as setting a limit on the number of messages an individual can send or having students use pseudonyms to mask their gender identities. Students may become student researchers who collaborate with the teacher researcher in designing a questionnaire to comment on each computer session to assess group dynamics (Pryor, 1995).

These recommendations are no different than those proposed by teacher researchers who have examined gender relations in oral forms of discussion (e.g., Gallas, 1995). Teachers must become action researchers in their own settings to determine if simply using electronic text can make discussions and writings more gender fair or, as in these studies, if other interventions are needed. In doing so, teachers may wish to experiment further with computer software programs that are designed to assist in electronic communications.

Recommendations for Research

These studies offer suggestions to expand this line of inquiry, from both their findings and their recommendations. First, these researchers have called for studies of how technology can mark identities and forge alliances, as well as subvert or reinforce power relations among students (Fey, 1998; Lewis & Fabos, 1999). Investigators such as Lewis and Fabos have pointed to the need to study and appreciate the lives and social literacies that students bring with them to school. In doing so, they caution, it will be necessary to create new pedagogies that incorporate new technologies and to offer critical frameworks for understanding them.

Second, more research should be done that explores electronic text as a medium for enhancing gender-fair communication. Some success in producing gender equity in discussions has been reported in the quantitative literature by using real-time, electronic collaborative-discussion tools in science classes (Hsi & Hoadley, 1997). This study, however, relied on tallies and self-reports and did not document or describe students' interactions through observations. In a similar study (McConnell, 1997), postgraduate students used a computer conferencing system, Caucas, to determine if this medium would allow more equality between the sexes in participation in discussion. Tallies of participation records showed that females did experience more turns, were able to speak for similar lengths of time as males, and were able to direct conversations. The researcher concluded, however, that this analysis was exploratory rather than confirmatory, and that the goals of the study, culture of the students, and local circumstances produced this result rather than technology.

Due to these disparate studies and the small number of such studies, more investigations are needed of gender and reading, writing, and discussion with electronic text, especially between same-sex groups. Researchers should document ways in which females (and males) are encouraged or discouraged from electronic communication, and researchers should explore ways to encourage voice in young women, particularly minority females, when using electronic forms of communication. Because the research on electronic communication is inconclusive, we recommend that teachers become action researchers in their own settings. More experimentation in classrooms is needed by teachers to become aware of the possibilities and limitations of electronic text to facilitate symmetrical opportunities for reading, writing, and discussion.

CHAPTER 6

Studies on Gender and Literacy Autobiography

Characteristics of the Studies

Thirteen studies were located that included or focused on gender in the analysis of literacy development and practice recorded in literacy autobiographies. Forty-six percent were literacy autobiographies written by authors of the studies (e.g., Erickson, Otto, et al., 1997; Hardenbrook, 1997; Jackson, 1989/1990, 1991), whereas 54% were analyses of literacy autobiographies gathered from others, usually for an undergraduate or graduate class (e.g., Duchein & Konopak, 1994; Gritsavage, 1997; Guzzetti, 1997). Ninety-two percent were life histories, while 8% were teacher action research. Of these studies, 47% were published.

Two studies (by one male researcher) were conducted in the United Kingdom, while 11 others (85%) were done in the United States. Seven literacy autobiographies were written by males (five of whom were prompted to do so for a session at the American Reading Forum). One literacy autobiography was written by an African American female. Ethnicity of the first author was stated in only 7% of the studies but could be inferred in 46% by familiarity with the researchers. Most researchers conducted their studies from multiple views. The most common frameworks were literacy as a social practice (69%), social constructivism (69%), and some type of feminism (69%), including social, Marxist, and black feminism. Of these studies, 96% were published.

The informants in the majority of the studies focused on European Americans (46%), while 22% focused on African Americans, Hispanics/Latinos, and foreign-born learners. All informants were adults and included 3% undergraduate students, 46% graduate students, or 51%

adults in the community. Informants tended to be middle class (39% of the studies) or working class (15% of the studies), with only 7% at the poverty or upper-class level. Of the studies, 38% of the studies focused on females only, whereas 15% included males only.

Themes

Four themes resulted from the analyses of these literacy autobiographies:

1. the gendered and social nature of literacy development
2. the social repercussions of literacy development
3. the influence of multiple subjectivities on literacy development
4. the potential and limits of literacy development

These themes are identified and exemplified in the following sections.

The Gendered and Social Nature of Literacy Development

Several authors wrote about how their own literacy development was regulated by their notions of what constituted appropriate reading materials for their gender. For example, in an article examining their literacy roots, Rick Erickson, Wayne Otto, Alice Randlett, Bernard Hayes, Tom Cloer, David Gustafson, and Ken Smith (1998) recalled male-oriented literacy sources, such as *Mad* magazine and stories in *Playboy*, which constituted peer-accepted reading for adolescent boys in the early 1960s. Erickson attributed these sources to providing him with a "lifelong passion for satire, humor, and good prose" (p. 212). Similarly, Bernard Hayes (in the same study) identified "Boy Books," baseball novels of the 1940s written by John R. Tunis. Hayes described these books as creating a world intuitively known to every boy who ever played catch with his father or listened to his grandfather's renditions of famous baseball games of yesterday. Hayes said of the books,

> But, more than any others, they exemplify the special ways in which sports books teach boys to read well. Perhaps Tunis knew this secret about boys and reading: It takes a game to know a game. Reading, like baseball, is something you have to play. (pp. 220–221)

Accordingly, Ken Smith, another Erickson colleague, recalled male figures in his reflections on his early literacy roots. He noted reading magazines aimed at boys, such as *Boy's Life*, and reading stories about male historical figures. He also reported reading male authors, such as Charles Dickens.

Another male researcher, David Jackson (1991), identified male comics as a gendered source of reading material for young men. A superhero, such as Captain Kidd, the single, powerful character of the story, was aimed at young boys' fantasies of achieving fully developed masculinity through physical strength and competition. These super-heroes were popular with young adolescent males who realized that their masculinity required them to be dominant, but who did not yet have the physical strength nor the social position to meet this expectation. Jackson recommended a critical rereading of superhero comics to reveal the ideological constructions of masculinity by attending to the distortions, omissions, and misrepresentations in the texts.

In addition to these reports by men, women also noted the gendered social nature of literacy development. For example, Paula Salvio (1995) described girls' covert readings of female authors, such as Judy Blume, who write about topics that cannot be discussed in the classroom without fear of embarrassment (like females' physical development). These female-oriented literacy sources can be secretly read by individual girls and shared among a group of girls. Salvio reported that girls were reduced to covert reading, which

> leaves young girls time for passing in the midst of the narrative, day-dreaming in between the lines of the text, imagining the possible implications these stories have for their lives and examining the words and images closely and critically. When girls covertly read romantic fiction, however, they are determined the opportunity to converse and write about their readings, including critical analysis of the contradictions between popular fiction's version of social relations and their own lives...young women become vulnerable to the culturally-sanctioned definition of femininity that plays on their feelings. (p. 12)

It follows then that young women readers consent to larger dominant patterns of power and control.

Ellen Brown (1993) also described the gendered nature of her own reading. She recalled her early reading of Hans Christian Anderson fairy tales in which women were portrayed as victims. She also described in later years to truly learning to read with Nancy Drew stories. She recalled,

> The reader of a Nancy book is never allowed to forget that our heroine—gunning down the highway after a gang of crooks—is a sweet young lady who dresses nicely and enjoys having tea with little cakes. (p. 6)

Nancy Drew lives in an affluent version of fairyland with a patriarchal figure, her father (her mother is deceased). Brown pointed out, however, that Nancy has been 18 years old for 60 years, and that her life is repetitive and formulaic. Although Nancy appears to be a Barbie with brains, breaking away from stereotypical female roles, in reality she is still contained by the world of her father, her freedom enabled only by an absent mother. Hence, these books present no strong image of a matriarch and provide restrictive images of appropriate feminine roles to young women.

One teacher researcher, Ann Berger-Knorr (1997), addressed the problem of gendered literacy development and practice by asking her preservice education students (21 white females; 1 Filipino/white female; and 4 white males from suburban or rural backgrounds) to write their educational autobiographies. She asked the students to reflect on how they were taught to read, and to share their thoughts about reading and reading instruction. The goal of the exercise was to provide a starting point for a project of unlearning privilege by providing the conditions for students to name their own experiences, to define their own realities, and then analyze how gender, race, and class played a role in shaping those realities. She asked her students to read an article on reading instruction and social class (Shannon,1985), an article on gender bias in the selection of children's literature (Luke, Cooke, & Luke, 1986), and an article on the language practices of black Americans (Heath, 1989). Next, students examined the experiences of subordinate groups in an attempt to connect with the lives of others and asked sensitive questions that would allow the students to empathize with those who were not so privileged. The final phase of the project asked students to reexamine their educational experiences in light of their gender, race, and class.

Only one student responded collectively to the categories of gender, race, and class. In doing so, a white female revealed that she knew very little about race, gender, and class bias. Almost half the students acknowledged their own social-class privilege and the ways in which it afforded them advantages over others, like attending private schools or traveling. In their discussions of ability grouping, however, these students demonstrated feeling the effects of a class system. For example, nine students recalled negative experiences in ability-grouped reading instruction and the stigmatization and embarrassment of being in the low group. Another student described how two second-grade classmates went to the third-grade classroom for reading instruction; this student did not think that was fair and subsequently was placed in the advanced reading group as a result of a parent complaint. A female student described how her mother, a first-grade teacher, started her reading books on her own and read with her nightly, a practice that helped her be placed in the top reading group.

In addition, the majority of children's stories mentioned in the autobiographies were male-dominated and presented monocultural, Eurocentric perspectives. All but three children's books were classified as either male-dominated, sexist, or racist. Based on these analyses, the students were asked to consider the assumptions that underlaid their selections and subsequent readings of these texts.

Discussions of these findings prompted these preservice teachers to become empowered to act on privilege in two ways. First, students openly denounced racist, sexist, and classist views. Second, they identified plans for incorporating curricular and instructional materials that better supported the experiences and interests of culturally diverse students. They also made plans to eliminate classroom practices, such as ability grouping, which initiate and maintain inequalities.

The Social Repercussions of Literacy Development

Two authors in three studies (Jackson, 1989/1990, 1991; Sohn, 1998) described the social ramifications and consequences of literacy development for males and females. In Katerine Sohn's (1998) analysis of college students' literacy autobiographies, students were classified as either confident or tentative literacy learners. Confident students had more to say about their literacy development. All were read to as children. Of these confident students, more women than men listed books they had collected, which numbered in the hundreds. The men tended to read horror novels and articles about installing car stereos. The women reported reading romantic novels, such as those by Danielle Steele. Women and their mothers used writing to sort out their personal feelings by keeping journals or diaries.

Despite these rich literacy histories, these confident students (and the tentative ones, also) expressed a desire to not appropriate a voice that would alienate them from their families. Sohn referred to the exercise of this voice as "getting above their raisin's" (p. 12). For when students learn a language that is culturally different than their own, along with the accompanying codes of power, they feel they may loose their cultural values. Sohn cautioned teachers to respond to the questions of alienation by blurring the dichotomies of insider-outsider language and examining the overlaps between the two.

David Jackson (1989/1990), a British male researcher, also described literacy development as alienation from family and former peers. One example he gave illustrated how his own expanding tastes in reading materials represented a sense of separation from his working-class family caused by his literacy development. Jackson described the mixed feelings he had when, at the age of 17, he gave his father a D.H. Lawrence novel for a Christmas present:

> It makes emotional sense now to reconstruct that episode as a complicated mixture of vindictive gloating that I'd gone far beyond him [his father] intellectually, and a regretful marker of the widening distance between us. (p.10)

Jackson described how gender and class relations became interwoven within his sense of linguistic distrust, anxiety, and awed reverence for the language of the educated. His motivation to acquire "impersonal, distanced Standard English" (p.13) was to prove his virility to his father. Jackson wrote of speaking with his father in intimate situations in his private language, and using his "boy wonder" language in competitive public contexts with patriarchal authorities (like his father) who seemed to reactivate his deeply compulsive sparring with his father:

> The possession of language also changed my customary relations with my parents. On one hand, language gave me a weapon to take on my father in the competition for my mother's love. I didn't have his relative authority or his physical strength, but I began to see that I could outshine him through my word power. And not just outshine, but put down

and humiliate in public. Out of these emotional origins came my language of competitive performance that has kept me on the partriarchal hook for a very long time. (p. 10)

Jackson learned to discard any distinguishing traces of home or street talk in official school contexts, accepting the public-private split in his life and the kinds of appropriate language that accompanied that split. Jackson also described "buddy boy" language, which he learned between the ages of 13 and 17. This particular vernacular was spoken in the nonadult public arena among males. It was a vernacular that characterized a boy as "one of the lads." Buddy boy language consisted of witty linguistic sparring—a way of getting closer to another boy while appearing to do the opposite—which increased solidarity of the bond among males in a group. Jackson identified this language as a substitute for the public impossibility of boys physically touching one another.

Jackson also described his own anxiety caused by competitive settings that impeded his ability to write. He identified the language of public prestige, in which scholars are announced by their credentials and current projects, as anxiety producing. This anxiety caused Jackson to remember the dislocations between his personal and public worlds, which inhibited the free flow of his academic writing.

The Influence of Multiple Subjectivities on Literacy Development

Five studies identified and described the influence of other layers or multiple subjectivities besides gender that influence literacy development (Gritsavage, 1997; Guzzetti, 1997; Hardenbrook, 1997; Jackson, 1989/1990, 1991). For example, in an analysis of graduate students' literacy autobiographies, Margaret Gritsavage (1997) identified the roles that social class and ethnicity played in these students' literacy development. For example, one student wrote of the influences of growing up poor and black in an inner-city neighborhood, such as learning a slang that emphasized males' use of expletives and toughness. In analyzing the students' talk about their literacy histories, Margaret found that generation also played a role in interaction with gender. For example, the oldest male student (who grew up in the 1940s) and the youngest female student (who grew up in the 1970s) had similar patterns of discourse and contributed most to discussions.

In a similar way, Barbara Guzzetti (1997) examined her graduate students' literacy autobiographies written in a graduate course. Analysis of these writings and students' subsequent discussions of their literacy histories revealed the interactive influence of geography and family with ethnicity and gender. For example, three autobiographers were Hispanics with backgrounds in the rural southwestern United States. Two of these autobiographers described the paucity of literacy models and resources available to them during their formative years. Both a Hispanic American male in his 50s and a Hispanic American female in her 30s recalled that they did not have any books at home (besides a set of encyclopedias). As youngsters, the male reported that his first exposure to books was at school; the female reported a lack of a print-rich home environment.

In another investigation of literacy life histories, Marie Hardenbrook (1997) identified the influence of life markers, or life stages, such as military service, personal crises, and illnesses, interacting with gender in literacy development and practice. For example, one European American, middle-class female wrote of contracting mononucleosis during first grade. Her illness confined her to bed where she spent several months reading, earning a stack of bookworm certificates from her teacher. In another example, an African American male became a serious reader while serving as an aircraft crew chief during military duty, following a tumultuous and difficult adolescence.

Mary Duchein and Bonnie Konopak (1992) also identified life markers like these. These researchers gathered literacy life histories from three retired women. These women were participants in a writer's workshop class for senior citizens, ages 62 to 80. Formal and informal interviews resulted in compositions of literacy life histories for each participant in her own words. Participants reviewed and then added to these autobiographies. From these literacy stories, Duchein and Konopak identified four life-span phases: (1) a preformal schooling phase, characterized by oral traditions and home settings that resulted in rich language development and provided models of literacy; (2) a formal schooling phase, in which memorable teachers and personal experiences in the home and community, such as library visits and out-of-school reading, influenced a love of literacy; (3) the homemaker or workplace phase in which reading and writing were integral parts of parenting or jobs; and (4) the retirement phase, characterized by a renewed interest in family stories and writing to fill a void produced by the death of a spouse or increased leisure time. Family literacy development seemed to go hand in hand with these responsibilities. In the fourth phase, writing poetry or prose provided a creative outlet and endowed women's lives with cohesion through retrospective awakenings in memories of events and people, providing vital historical and personal legacies for future generations. Duchein and Konopak concluded that although it was impossible to separate literacy practices from the myriad complexities of life itself, these life histories revealed the importance of the school in fostering personal and motivational aspects of literacy.

The Potential and Limits of Literacy Development

Two studies (Bassard, 1992; Geissler, 1986) were historical analyses of 19th-century women's literacy development, as revealed through their writings and autobiographies. In examining the literacy of African American women of the past, Katherine Clay Bassard (1992) noted that literacy historically had been about the interplay between power and knowledge. Unfortunately, these African American women (e.g., Amanda Berry Smith, 1893; Harriet Jacobs, 1861; Jarenea Lee, 1849) were marginalized on the basis of both their gender and their race, causing them to be "keenly aware of the limits of the literacy-as-freedom ideology" (p. 120). They were forced to self-publish and were afraid to sell their writings to others—not exactly fulfilling the promise of literacy as economic and social advancement. Their development as readers and writers also proved to be dangerous when others forced texts on them. For example, Linda Brent, a former slave, described the experience of having a man make sexual advances to her through notes. Brent lied about her ability to read these notes as a way to protect herself from sordid material. This turned out to be an ineffectual attempt, as these notes were simply read to her instead. Hence, literacy development for women who were former slaves did not result in the kinds of freedoms they had imagined or that society had promised.

Kathleen Geissler (1986) conducted another study that examined the social meaning of women's literacy in the 60 years following the American Revolution. Like Bassard, she also addressed the ideologies and social consequences of literacy development for women by examining the autobiographies of four women writers: Maria Foster Brown, Lucy Larcom, Jane Grey Swisshelm, and Elizabeth Oakes Smith. Two of these women described the tension between literacy and gender roles in their autobiographies. For example, although women's literacy rates had doubled, gender role expectations limited the extent to which women like Swisshelm (who resorted to using pseudonyms) were able to write and publish, as well as read for pleasure. Swisshelm's 1880 autobiography revealed constraints placed on her literacy development, particularly public speaking, by the marginal community of her husband's family, the Methodist church, and the cultural perceptions of women's roles. Similarly, Smith's (undated) autobiography revealed the conflict between her mother's desire for Smith to marry early versus Smith's own desire for a career as a poet, identifying the constraints of sociocultural context on her literacy development.

Discussion

Four themes resulted from our examination of studies on gender and literacy autobiography: (1) the gendered and social nature of literacy development, (2) the social repercussions of literacy development, (3) the influence of multiple subjectivities on literacy development, and (4) the potential and limits of literacy development.

The first theme, the gendered and social nature of literacy development, was noted through the reflective self-revelations that participants made in their literacy autobiographies. These researchers revealed themselves and the impact this reflective and critical process had on them as researchers, more so than investigators in other lines of inquiry in this review.

The second theme, the social repercussions of literacy development, drew from experiences of past and present literacy learners. Because we think of literacy development as beneficial, it is often surprising to discover the social consequences of people "getting above their raisin's" (Sohn,1998). These stories suggest that new generations who develop their literacy abilities and interests very well may be alienating themselves from their families and peers as they do so. This theme reminds us that literacy development may have costs as well as benefits.

The third theme, the influence of multiple subjectivities on literacy development, was taken from exemplary studies that show, through participants' self-revelations, the importance of multiple layers (e.g., race, social class, generation) that influence and interact with gender in the development of literacies. In particular, these studies illustrate the impossibility of separating the influence of only one of these subjectivities without taking into account the others that are interwoven with gender. By identifying these multiple layers, these researchers alluded to the dangers of essentializing. In doing so, they remind us as researchers of gender and literacies of the importance of describing both ourselves as researchers and our informants as participants when we report our investigations.

The fourth theme, the potential and limits of literacy development, relates to the second theme of social consequences due to literacy development, by reminding us that literacy development does not automatically result in improved social or economic conditions. Historically, gender role expectations have limited women's opportunities. Both religion and family have placed constraints on women's literate practices and performances. Although not as widespread now as it was in the 19th century, women in the United States still face marginalization in careers that require high levels of literacy, such as academics and law. Therefore, literacy development does not always bring literacy success, even today.

Recommendations for Instruction

Because of the nature of the self-revelations and self-realizations in these literacy autobiographies, we recommend the practice of students writing their own literacy autobiographies. We suggest teacher modeling and students practicing writing literacy autobiographies, and encouraging reflective examinations as critical literacy activities. We believe that doing so will allow students the opportunity for self-realization and will perhaps interrupt the development and maintenance of gendered literacy practices.

Recommendations for Research

Little research has been conducted on the process and results of writing literacy autobiographies. More research is needed that not only analyzes the content of literacy autobiographies, but also examines the students' reactions to writing their literacy life histories. Researchers should investigate the process of reflection and students' metacognitive awareness and realizations as they author their literacy stories. We also need to know if and how authorship results in students' increased awareness of their gendered literacy practices and what impact their self-realizations have on their future choices.

CHAPTER 7

Cross-Genre Summary, Recommendations, and Reflections

Cross-Genre Characteristics of the Studies

In total, we located 128 qualitative studies in 129 reports that addressed gender and literacies. This line of inquiry began in the mid-1980s and has increasingly continued into the 21st century. The growing number of investigations reflects increased interest in and attention to the issue of gender as an influence on the development and practice of literacies. Most of these studies were conducted in the United States (77%), but researchers in other nations, including the United Kingdom (10%) and Canada (9%), also contributed to this line of inquiry. Most researchers in these studies were European American females, 57% of whom were first authors. Forty-one percent of the researchers did not state their gender or ethnicity. The most common theoretical frame used in the studies was literacy as a social practice (41%). More than half (56%) the studies were published.

In many cases, authors did not state the ethnicity, social class, or gender of their participants. When ethnicity was stated, 42% of participants were identified as European Americans, and 11% were identified as African Americans. Ethnicity was not stated for 34% of participants. The socioeconomic status of participants was 38% middle class or upper middle class, and 28% of participants were working poor or poverty level. Participants were mostly elementary (30%) or middle or junior high students (34%). When gender was stated, 46% of studies included participants of both genders. In only 13% of the studies were participants active in contributing to the research process.

Cross-Genre Themes

We were able to discover patterns in practices that constrain students across genres of studies, providing strong and collective evidence of the existence of the phenomenon individual researchers observed. One theme we identified was oppression and marginalization of females in literacy learning. For example, in both discussion studies (Guzzetti, 1996a, 1996b) and writing studies (Blair, 1996, 1998; Henkin, 1995), females rarely shared their ideas (in written or oral forms) for fear of boys' negative responses, such as criticisms and teasing.

A second theme in both the gender and reading and gender and writing studies was freedom. In the writing studies, it was the freedom of writers' workshop in topic selection. In the reading studies, it was the free choice of book selections and unstructured literature response for reacting to those selections. Each of these freedoms, however, may actually constrain students by reinforcing their gendered identities and literacy practices. See Cherland (1992, 1994) for a discussion of reader response, Hunt (1995) for a discussion of free-choice writing, and Luce-Kapler (1999) for a discussion of free-choice versus teacher-selected literature.

A third theme across the genres was the difficulties associated with attempts to interrupt gendered practices. We found this theme in all the genres of studies. Students resisted attempts to change asymmetrical participation for several reasons. Either it was not their own agenda to do so, or they hesitated because of the risks and benefits associated with maintaining the status quo.

A fourth theme that crossed genres was that although disrupting gendered practice may be difficult, it is not impossible. Interventions that showed some success included grouping by gender in the discussion and writing studies, using pseudonyms in the studies of electronic communications, and critical questioning and careful choice of texts that defy gender stereotypes in the reading studies.

Recommendations for Teachers and Teacher Educators

These studies have offered some classroom-tested ways to address the problem of gendered participation in literacy practices. Three of these strategies were recommended in studies from more than one genre. The first of these was recommended in all the genres. This strategy has dual components: to increase students' awareness of gender disparity, and to involve students in addressing the problem. The second part of this strategy is most important because simply raising awareness of the problem might only serve to reinforce the problem.

Ways to raise awareness and address the problem included incorporating critical literacy activities, tracing participation records, teaching discourse analysis techniques, and facilitating metacommunication. For example, Karen Gallas (1995) reported success with metacommunication (students talking about their talk) to address gender inequities and power imbalances with elementary students. Researchers such as Carole Edelsky and Susan Harman (1991) suggested teaching discourse analysis techniques to help students understand the relationships between gender and language by analyzing closely words and phrases in text and talk. Young (2000) reported some success in challenging gender stereotypes that affect interpretations of texts by using critical literacy activities and teaching students to read against text. In addition, writing literacy autobiographies raised awareness of gendered literacy development. Marion Fey (1998) demonstrated that electronic discussions might be more gender fair when the context and content of those discussions promotes awareness of and attention to feminist issues and gendered literacy practices.

A second recommendation that we found in studies of both gender and discussion and gender and writing was to place students in same-sex groups. For example, Guzzetti (1996b) reported that effective discussions occurred in high school classrooms when those discussions were structured by gender. Karen Evans (1999) found that the most successful literature-discussion groups of elementary students were those in which the students were in same-sex groups. Brett Elizabeth Blake (1997) found that all-girl writing groups at the elementary level provided a safe and conducive environment for females to share their writing. When given the choice, females in these studies usually preferred same-sex groups.

A third recommendation that crossed genres was exposure to a wide variety of texts and reading materials, which included poetry, essays, plays, and books with unconventional themes and nontraditional language. Researchers in reading studies recommended allowing access to alternative reading materials, such as comic books, 'zines, and websites. Researchers in writing studies suggested experimenting with students' writing in different literacy forms, such as narratives, poetry, and plays.

Recommendations for Researchers

The ways in which these studies generally have been conducted may serve to work against the goal of literacy for all. Researchers most often chose privileged groups—European Americans (44%) from middle-class families (36%) as informants. A related oversight in all the studies was researchers' tendency to neglect to describe the largest percentage of informants' ethnicity in 34% of the studies, participants' socioeconomic class in 34% of the studies, and gender in 21% of the studies. These omissions lead to the danger of "essentializing"—believing that all females and all males are alike in their gendered literacies and, for example, that generalizations can be made from observations of the racial majority to those of racial minority or other socioeconomic classes. We have evidence, for instance, from studies that focused on African Americans that females in predominantly African American and middle-class classrooms participate much more freely in whole-class discussions than do European American females in predominantly middle-class and European American classrooms. Hence, social justice cannot be obtained for all students until we understand how all students are disenfranchised or marginalized in their literacy performances.

When taken as a whole, these studies fall short of expectations for feminist research or for studies that should exemplify feminist frameworks. As Stanley and Wise (1993) caution, feminist researchers should examine and describe their own identities, experiences, attitudes, and values that affect the research. Qualitative feminist researchers should also make explicit the ways in which they affected and were affected by the research. As a whole, these researchers neglected to fill these requirements. For example, the first author's gender was not stated and could not be inferred in 37% of the 128 studies. The first author's ethnicity was not stated in 83% of these studies. These descriptive statistics are indicators of how researchers revealed little information about themselves in their studies. Hence, we know little about the researchers' filters that affected the research other than their theoretical frames. In addition, only a handful of researchers described how the research affected them.

Our analysis of the silences, suggestions, and unanswered questions in these studies provides us with direction for future research. First, we recommend that more focus be placed on students from a wide range of ethnicities and from lower socioeconomic classes. We originally intended to conduct a review of the literature on the influence of gender and culture on literacies. We found, however, that few studies addressed both aspects of participants' identities. Hence, our review is constrained by the limitations of the existing research. As Carl Grant and Christine Sleeter (1986) discovered in their review of educational research, race, class, and gender are seldom integrated in studies, but are treated as separate influences. These researchers, like we do, make a case for integration of multiple subjectivities in research.

We also call for researchers to reveal more of themselves in the conduct and analysis of their investigations. Doing so would facilitate a more informed interpretation of their findings. We also ask researchers to describe how they affected and were affected by the research. For example, why do some researchers lose interest in interrupting gendered discursive practices and turn their attentions elsewhere to other lines of inquiry? Do those conducting feminist projects aimed at intervention become discouraged by their results? What are the most promising and hopeful aspects of these efforts?

Fourth, we call for researchers to expand their roles by forming partnerships with the teachers in whose classrooms they are investigating. We also call for teachers to become action researchers in their own classrooms and conduct more studies that are teacher research. We have tried to describe these studies with enough specificity to permit teachers to attempt these methods in their own classrooms to conduct observations and intervene in gendered literacy practices. The studies we reviewed provide a clear picture of the ways in which gender disparity shows up in literacy learning and practice. It is time now to turn attention to ways to address the problem in other contexts.

Finally, we hope to see more studies that involve students as student researchers and problem solvers. Although these studies showed that simply talking with students about the problem may only serve to reinforce it, we know little about what happens when students are asked to take an active part in addressing the problem. Therefore, we would like to see more studies of students being involved in creating and employing solutions to gendered literacy practices.

Our Reflections

The process of reading and reflecting on these studies reinforces our belief that it is important to build students' awareness of how language constructs gender. We also now more firmly believe that it is important to offer students opportunities to explore gendered identities in and through reading, writing, and discussion. We have become aware more fully of the difficulty yet the necessity of helping students to deconstruct categories of male and female.

We leave this review hopeful for the future. We have identified the types of questions that we anticipate future researchers may address in their inquiries. More complete information will allow us additional insights into the development of and practices in literacies. We cannot provide "literacy and justice for all" (Edelsky & Harman, 1991) until we know how this is best accomplished for the diverse students that teachers face each day. It is our hope that this synthesis will provide teachers with the impetus to become action researchers in their own classrooms and will provide direction to university researchers to form partnerships with teachers to continue and extend this work for social change.

Can such change be made despite the risks the researchers identified? Critical theorists such as Giroux (1995) believe so, stating that feminist theories and pedagogies

> offer new hope for educators who believe that schools can still be changed and that their individual and collective actions can make a difference in extending democracy and social justice in the wider society. (p. 35)

Perhaps when more studies of and interventions into gender and literacies are conducted with an emancipatory agenda, more efforts will result in "justice for all" in classroom language and literacy. By acting to change what is oppressive, Edelsky and Harman (1991) believe that teachers and learners may "join together into a new community sharing a common responsibility for effecting change" (p. 138). We hope that our review will in some way assist in facilitating that change.

Bibliography of Studies on Gender and Discussion

Alvermann, D.E. (1993, December). Student voice in class discussion: A feminist poststructuralist perspective. In D.E. Alvermann (Chair), *Expanding the possibilities: How feminist theories inform traditions and positions in reader response, classroom discussion, and critical thinking.* Symosium presented at the annual meeting of the National Reading Conference, Charleston, SC.

Alvermann, D. (1995). Peer-led discussions: Whose interests are served? *Journal of Adolescent & Adult Literacy, 39,* 282–289.

Alvermann, D.E., Commeyras, M., Young, J.P., Randall, S., & Hinson, D. (1997). Interrupting gendered discursive practices in classroom talk about texts: Easy to think about, difficult to do. *Journal of Literacy Research, 29*(1), 73–104.

Alvermann, D.E., Young, J.P., & Green, C. (1997). *Adolescents' negotiations of out-of-school reading discussions* (Reading Research Report No. 77). Athens, GA: National Reading Research Center.

Cherland, M.R. (1992). Gendered readings: Cultured restraints upon response to literature. *The New Advocate, 5*(3), 187–197.

Evans, K.S. (1999, April). Fifth-grade students' discussion groups. Paper presented at the annual meeting of the American Educational Research Association, Montreal, Canada.

Evans, K.S., Alvermann, D., & Anders, P.L. (1998). Literature discussion groups: An examination of gender roles. *Reading Research and Instruction, 37*(2), 107–122.

Gallas, K. (1995). *Talking their way into science: Hearing children's questions and theories, responding with curricula.* New York: Teachers College Press.

Gritsavage, M. (1997a). *Examining dominance in discourse in the graduate course, Gender, Culture and Literacy.* Unpublished manuscript, Arizona State University, Tempe.

Gritsavage, M. (1997b, December). *Gendered discourse in classroom conversations about gender, culture, and literacy.* Paper presented at the annual meeting of the National Reading Conference, Scottsdale, AZ.

Guzzetti, B.J. (2001). Texts and talk: The role of gender in learning physics. In E.B. Moje & D. O'Brien (Eds.), *Constructions of literacy: Studies of teaching and learning literacy in secondary classrooms* (pp. 125–146). Mahwah, NJ: Erlbaum.

Guzzetti, B.J., & Williams, W.O. (1996a). Changing the pattern of gendered discussion: Lessons from science classrooms. *Journal of Adolescent & Adult Literacy, 40,* 2–11.

Guzzetti, B.J., & Williams, W.O. (1996b). Gender, text, and discussion: Examining intellectual safety in the science classroom. *Journal of Research in Science Teaching, 33,* 5–20.

Hinchman, K.A., & Young, J.P. (1996, April). *Resistance and acquiescence in text-based classroom talk.* Paper presented at the annual meeting of the American Educational Research Association, New York, NY.

Holden, C. (1993). Giving girls a chance: Patterns of talk in cooperative group work. *Gender and Education, 5*(2), 179–189.

Kyle, S. (1997). *Discussion patterns of African American students in classroom discourse.* Unpublished manuscript, Arizona State University, Tempe.

Luster, B., Varelas, M., Wenzel, S., & Liao, J. (1997, March). *Race and gender in the classroom: Perspectives from school-based and university-based researchers.* Paper presented at the annual meeting of the American Educational Research Association, Chicago, IL.

Marks, T. (1995). Gender differences in third graders' oral discourse during peer led literature discussion groups (Doctoral dissertation, University of Maryland, 1995). *Dissertation Abstracts International, 56-08A,* 2997. (A19539701)

Meyer, D.K., & Fowler, L.A. (1993, December). *Is gender related to classroom discourse across content areas?* Paper presented at the annual meeting of the National Reading Conference, Charleston, SC.

Moore, D.W. (1997). Some complexities of gendered talk about texts. *Journal of Literacy Research, 29*(4), 507–530.

Morrison, D.F.G. (1995). Introducing critical literacy in the classroom: A teacher's search (Doctoral dissertation, University of New Brunswick, 1995). *Dissertation Abstracts International, 34*(5), 1735. (AAT MM06947)

Nelson, K.A. (1990). Gender communication through small groups. *English Journal,* 58–61.

Norris-Handy, J. (1996). *Voices under the volcano: An inquiry into silencing, gender and relation in a middle school classroom.* Unpublished master's thesis, Pacific Lutheran University, Tacoma, WA.

O'Donnell-Allen C., & Smagorinsky, P. (1999). Revising Ophelia: Rethinking questions of gender and power in school. *English Journal, 88*(3), 35–42.

O'Flahavan, J. (1989). *Second graders' social, intellectual, and affective development in varied group discussions about narrative texts: An exploration of participation.* Unpublished doctoral dissertation, University of Illinois, Urbana-Champaign.

Phelps, S., & Weaver, D. (1999). Public and personal voice in adolescents' classroom talk. *Journal of Literacy Research, 31*(3), 321–354.

Smith, S.A. (1998). Texts, transactions and talk: Early adolescent girls construction of meaning in a literature discussion group (Doctoral dissertation, New York University, 1998). *Dissertation Abstracts International, 59*(05), 1495. (AAT 9832770)

Tannen, D. (1986). *That's not what I meant: How conversational style makes or breaks relationships.* New York: Ballentine.

Tannen, D. (1990). *You just don't understand: Women and men in conversation.* New York: Ballentine.

Tannen, D. (1992). How men and women use language differently in their lives and in the classroom. *Education Digest, 57,* 3–9.

Tannen, D. (1995). The power of talk: Who gets heard and why. *Harvard Business Review, 73*(5), 138–148.

Tolmie, H., & Howe, C. (1993). Gender and dialogue in secondary school physics. *Gender and Education, 5*(2), 191–209.

Wilkinson, L.C., Lindow, J., & Chang, C. (1985). Sex differences and sex segregation in students' small-group communication. In L.C. Wilkinson & C.B. Marrett (Eds.), *Gender influences in classroom interaction* (pp. 185–205). Madison, WI: University of Wisconsin.

Wilson, J., & Haug, B. (1995). Collaborative modeling and talk in the classroom. *Language and Education, 9*(4), 265–281.

Young, J.P. (2000). Boy talk: Critical literacies and masculinities. *Reading Research Quarterly, 35, 312–337.*

Bibliography of Studies on Gender and Reading

Bardsley, D. (1999). *Boys and reading: What reading fiction means to sixth grade boys*. Unpublished doctoral dissertation, Arizona State University, Tempe.

Barrow, I., Broaddus, K., & Crook, P. (1995). Lenses of gender, experience, and age: Revealing personal connections to literature. *Perspectives on Literacy Research and Practice, 44*, 289–294.

Beach, R. (1995). Constructing cultural models through response to literature. *English Journal, 84*(6), 87–94.

Benjamin, B., & Irwin-DeVitis, L. (1998). Censoring girls choices: Continued gender bias in English language arts classrooms. *English Journal, 87*(2), 64–71.

Blair, H., & Reschny, S. (1995). Girls, girls, girls: The voice of women in adolescent literature. *Query, 25*(1), 52–57.

Blair, H., & Sanford, K. (1999, November). *Boys will be boys: Expanding literacy horizons for boys*. Paper presented at annual meeting of the National Council of Teachers of English, Denver, CO.

Broughton, M.A. (1998). Early adolescent girls and their reading practices: Refection and transformation of subjectivities through experiences with literature (Doctoral dissertation, University of Georgia, 1998). *Dissertation Abstracts International, 59*(06), 1948. (AAT 9836306)

Brown, J. (1997). New heroes: Gender, race, fans and comic book superheroes (Doctoral dissertation, University of Toronto, Canada, 1998). *Dissertation Abstracts International, 59*(06), 1818. (AAT NQ27882)

Cherland, M.R. (1992). Gendered readings: Cultured restraints upon response to literature. *The New Advocate, 5*(3), 187–197.

Cherland, M.R. (1994). *Private practices: Girls reading fiction and constructing identity*. London: Taylor & Francis.

Cherland, M.R., & Edelsky, C. (1993). Girls and reading: The desire for agency and the horror of helplessness in fictional encounters. In L.C. Smith (Ed.), *Texts of desire: Essays on fiction, femininity and schooling* (28–43). Washington, DC: Falmer Press.

Christian-Smith, L.K. (1993a). *Texts of desire: Essays on fiction, femininity and schooling*. London; Washington, DC: Falmer Press.

Christian-Smith, L.K. (1993b). Voices of resistance: Young women readers of romance fiction. In L. Weis & M. Fine (Eds.), *Class, race, and gender in United States schools* (pp. 169–189). Albany, NY: State University of New York Press.

Danridge, J. (1999, December). *Discovering the heart soul of literacy: Exploring literate cultural identity construction in an African-American women's book club*. Paper presented at the annual meeting of the National Reading Conference, Orlando, FL.

Davies, B. (1991). *Frogs and snails and feminist tales: Preschool children and gender*. North Sydney, Australia: Allen & Unwin.

Davies, B. (1993). *Shards of glass: Children reading and writing beyond gendered identities*. Cresskill, NJ: Hampton Press.

DeBlase-Trzyna, G. (1999). *Classroom literacy and the textual formation of gender: Urban girls constructing social identities*. Unpublished doctoral dissertation, University of New York, Buffalo.

Dressman, M. (1997). Preference as performance: Doing social class and gender in three school libraries. *Journal of Literacy Research, 29*(3), 319–361.

Ferrell, J. (1998). The influence of gender on the interpretation and creation of texts (Doctoral dissertation, Southern Illinois University at Carbondale, 1999). *Dissertation Abstracts International, 59*(08), 2960. (UMI 9902720)

Finders, M. (1996). Queens and teen zines: Early adolescent females reading their way toward adulthood. *Anthropology & Educational Quarterly, 27*(1), 71–89.

Flynn, E.A. (1983). Gender and reading. *College English, 45*(3), 236–253.

Gonzalez, N.L. (1997). Nancy Drew: Girls' literature, women's reading groups, and the transmission of literacy. *Journal of Literacy Research, 29*(2), 221–251.

Hanley, B.L. (1998). Gender and reading: A study of the reading response patterns of two female and two male college students (Doctoral dissertation, University of Georgia, 1998). *Dissertation Abstracts International, 59*(06), 1965. (AAT 9836321)

Johnson, H.A. (1997). Reading the personal and the political: Exploring female representation in realistic fiction with adolescents (Doctoral dissertation, University of Arizona, 1997). *Dissertation Abstracts International, 58*(11), 4212. (AAT 981443)

Johnson, H.A., & Fox, D.L. (1998). Adolescent girls' responses to female literary characters: Two case studies. In A.C. Goodwyn (Ed.), *Literacy and media texts in secondary English: New approaches* (pp. 110–128). London: Cassell.

Leroy, C.A. (1995). Opposition and literacy among girls in an inner-city classroom (Doctoral dissertation, University of Alberta, 1995). *Dissertation Abstracts International, 57*(03A), 1025. (AAT NN06245)

Mallett, M. (1997). Gender and genre: Reading and writing choices of older juniors. *Reading, 31*(2), 48–57.

Millard, E. (1994). *Developing readers in the middle years.* Buckingham, UK; Philadelphia: Open University Press.

Millard, E. (1997). Differently literate: Gender identity and the construction of the developing reader. *Gender and Education, 9*(1), 31–48.

Nauman, A. (1997). Reading boys, reading girls: How sixth graders understand and are influenced by fictional characters (Doctoral dissertation, University of Illinois at Chicago, 1997). *Dissertation Abstracts International, 58*(04), 1234. (AAT 9728537)

Osmont, P. (1987). Teacher inquiry in the classroom: Reading and gender set. *Language Arts, 64*(7), 758–761.

Pace, B., & Townsend, J. (1999). Gender roles: Listening to classroom talk about literacy characters. *English Journal, 88*(3), 43–49.

Prosenjak, N. (1997). *How middle school readers respond as gendered readers of gendered texts.* Unpublished doctoral dissertation, Kent State University, Kent, OH.

Rice, P. (2000). Gendered readings of a traditional feminist folktale by sixth-grade boys and girls. *Journal of Literacy Research, 32*(2), 211–236.

Rigg, P. (1985). Petra: Learning to read at 45. *Journal of Education, 67*(1), 129–139.

Silliman, B. (1997). Four girls respond to young adult horror fiction. *Dissertation Abstracts International, 58*(9), 3461. (UMI 9810294)

Wheeler, M.A. (1984). Fourth grade boys' literacy from a mother's point of view. *Language Arts, 61*(6), 607–615.

Willinsky, J., & Hunniford, M.R. (1993). Reading the romance younger: The mirrors and fears of a preparatory literature. In L. Smith (Ed.), *Texts of desire: Essays on fiction, femininity and schooling* (pp. 87–105). Washington, DC: Falmer Press.

Wing, A. (1997). How can children be taught to read differently? *Bill's New Frock* and the "hidden curriculum." *Gender and Education, 9*(4), 491–504.

Bibliography of Studies on Gender and Writing

Blair, H. (1996). *Gender and discourse: Adolescent girls construct gender through talk and text.* Unpublished doctoral dissertation, University of Arizona, Tucson. Also as Blair, H. (2000). Genderlects: Girl talk in a middle years language arts classroom. *Language Arts, 77*(2), 315–323.

Blake, B.E. (1997). *She say, he say! Urban girls write their lives.* Albany, NY: State University of New York Press.

Brodkey, L. (1989). On the subjects of class and gender in "the literacy letters." *College English, 54*, 125–141.

Brown, V.A. (1997). *Treasure from our trash: A study of unofficial, vernacular literacy among sixth graders* (Report No. CS 215 919). Portions of paper presented at the annual meeting of the American Educational Research Association, Chicago, IL. (ERIC Document Reproduction Service No. ED 410 571)

Burdick, T. (1997). Snakes and snails and puppy dog tails: Girls and boys expressing voice. *Youth Services in Libraries, Fall*, 28–35.

Cleary, L.M. (1996). "I think I know what my teachers want now": Gender and writing motivation. *English Journal, 85*(1), 50–57.

Comber, B., & Kamler, B. (1997). Politicizing the literacy classroom. *Interpretations 30*(1), 30–53

Dyson, A.H. (1994). Theninjas, the X-men, and the ladies: Playing with power and identity in an urban primary school. *Teachers College Record, 96*(2), 219–239.

Dyson, A.H. (1995). The courage to write: Childing meaning making in a contested world. *Language Arts, 72*, 324–333.

Dyson, A.H. (1997). *Writing superheroes: Contemporary childhood, popular culture and classroom literacy.* New York: Teachers College Press.

Fiesta, M.J. (1997). Performing gender in the writing classroom: to refuse authority, to disperse authority, or to claim authority? *Arizona English Bulletin, 39*(2), 20–29.

Finders, M.J. (1996). "Just girls": Literacy and allegiance in junior high school. *Written Communication, 13*(1), 93–129.

Fleming, S. (1995). Whose stories are validated? *Language Arts, 72,* 590–596.

Fox, T. (1986). Method and gender-related motives in reading and writing. *Forum in Reading and Language Education,* 7–78.

Graves, D. (1975). An examination of the writing process of seven-year-old children. *Research in the Teaching of English, 9*(3), 227–241.

Harper, H. (1998). Dangerous desires: Feminist literacy criticism in a high school writing class. *Theory Into Practice, 37,* 220–228.

Harper, H.J. (1995). *Danger at the borders: The response of high school girls to feminist writing practices.* Unpublished doctoral dissertation, University of Toronto, Ontario.

Haswell, J., & Haswell, R.H. (1995). Gendership and the miswriting of students. *College Composition and Communication, 46*(2), 223–254.

Henkin, R. (1995, October). Insiders and outsiders in first-grade writing workshops: Gender and equity issues. *Language Arts, 72,* 429–434.

Henry, A. (1998). "Speaking up" and "speaking out": Examining "voice" in a reading/writing program with African Caribbean girls. *Journal of Literacy Research, 30*(2), 233–252.

Howe, F. (1984). *Myths of coeducation: Selected essays, 1964–1983.* Bloomington, IN: Indiana University Press.

Hunt, S. (1995). Choice in the writing class: How do students decide what to write and how to write it? *The Quarterly of the National Writing Project and the Center for the Study of Writing, 17*(2), 7–11.

Kamler, B. (1993). Construction gender in the process writing classroom. *Language Arts, 70,* 95–102.

Kamler, B. (1994). Gender and genre in early writing. *Linguistics and Education, 6,* 153–182.

Laidlaw, L. (1998). Finding "real" lives: Writing and identity. *Language Arts, 75*(2), 126–128.

Luce-Kapler, R. (1999). As if women writing. *Journal of Literacy Research, 31,* 267–291.

MacGillivray, L., & Martinez, A.M. (1998). Princesses who commit suicide: Primary children writing within and against gender stereotypes. *Journal of Literacy Research, 30*(1), 53–84.

Maher, A., Wade, B., & Moore, M. (1997). 'Goslob is a boy's name.' *English in Education, 31*(1), 24–35.

McAuliffe, S. (1993/1994). Toward understanding one another: Second graders' use of gendered language and story styles. *The Reading Teacher, 47,* 302–310.

Meinhof, U.H. (1997). "The most important event of my life!" A comparison of male and female written narratives. In S. Johnson & U.H. Meinhof (Eds.), *Language and Masculinity* (pp. 208–228). Cambridge, MA: Blackwell.

Moss, G. (1993). The place for romance in young people's writing. In L.K. Christian-Smith (Ed.), *Texts of desire: Essays in fiction, femininity, and schooling* (pp. 106–125). Washington, DC: Falmer Press.

Norris-Handy, J.B. (1996). *Voices under the volcano: An inquiry into silencing, gender, and relation in a middle school classroom.* Unpublished masters thesis, Pacific Lutheran University, Tacoma, WA.

Orellana, M.F. (1995). Literacy as a gendered social practice: Tasks, texts, talk and take up. *Reading Research Quarterly, 30,* 674–708.

Osborn, S. (1991). "Revision/re-vision": A feminist writing class. *Rhetoric Review, 9*(2), 258–273.

Peterson, S. (1998). Evaluation and teachers' perceptions of gender in sixth-grade student writing. *Research in the Teaching of English, 33,* 181–208.

Peterson, S. (1999, December). *Gendered subjectivities and personal expression in middle-grade writing: What are the possibilities?* Paper presented at the annual meeting of the National Reading Conference, Orlando, FL.

Phinney, M.Y. (1994). Gender, status, writing and the resolution of kindergarten girls' social tensions. *Linguistics and Education, 6,* 311–330.

Rich, A. (1979). *On lies, secrets, and silence: Selected prose.* New York: Norton

Roen, D.H. (1992). Gender and teacher response to student writing. In N.M. McCracken & B.C. Apple (Eds.), *Gender Issues in the Teaching of English* (pp. 126–141). Portsmouth, NH: Boynton/Cook.

Scarboro, C.B. (1994). *Writing and difference: The student, gender, and the text* (Report No. CS 214 803). Paper presented at the annual meeting of the Mid-South Educational Research Association, Nashville, TN. (ERIC Document Reproduction Service No. ED381793)

Schultz, K. (1996). Between school and work: The literacies of urban adolescent females. *Anthropology & Education Quarterly, 27*(4), 517–544.

Simmons, J. (1997). Attack of the killer baby faces: Gender similarities in third-grade writing. *Language Arts, 74,* 116–123.

Simon, L. (1997). *Making worlds from words: An analysis of the oral and written narratives of a preadolescent girl.* Paper presented at the annual meeting of the American Educational Research Association, Chicago, IL.

Utley, O.M., & Mathews, C. (1996). *The effects of teacher prompts on gender and comprehension.* (ERIC Document Reproduction Service No. 418941)

Waff, D.R. (1994). Girl talk: Creating community through social exchange. In M. Fine (Ed.), *Chartering urban school reform: Reflections on public high schools in the midst of change* (pp. 192–203). New York: Teachers College Press.

Wheeler, M.A. (1985). Using print socially—choosing books and writing notes in a fifth grade. *Dissertation Abstracts International, 46*(08), 2251. (AAT 8523466)

Widerberg, K. (1998). Teaching gender through writing. "Experience stories." *Women's Studies International Forum, 2*(2), 193–198.

Bibliography of Studies on Gender and Electronic Text

Christie, A. (1995). *No chips on their shoulders: Girls, boys and telecommunications*. Unpublished doctoral dissertation, Arizona State University, Tempe.

Fey, M. (1997). Literate behavior in a cross-age computer-mediated discussion: A question of empowerment. In C. Kinzer, K. Hinchman, & D. Leu (Eds.), *Inquiries in literacy theory and practice: Forty-sixth yearbook of the National Reading Conference* (pp. 507–518). Chicago: National Reading Conference.

Fey, M. (1998). Critical literacy in school-college collaboration through computer networking: A feminist research project. *Journal of Literacy Research*, *30*(1), 85–117.

Lewis, C., & Fabos, B. (1999, December). *Chatting on-line: Uses of instant message communication among adolescent girls*. Paper presented at the annual meeting of the National Reading Conference, Orlando, FL.

Nicholson, J., Gelpi, A., Young, S., & Sulzby, E. (1998). Influences of gender and open-ended software on first graders' collaborative composing activities on computers. *Journal of Computing in Childhood Education*, *9*(1), 3–42.

Pryor, J. (1995). Gender issues in groupwork—a case study involving computers. *British Educational Research Journal*, *21*(3), 277–287.

Bibliography of Studies on Gender and Literacy Autobiography

Bassard, K.C. (1992). Gender and genre: Black women's autobiography and the ideology of literacy. *African American Review, 26*(1), 119–129.

Berger-Knorr, A.L. (1998). Unlearning privilege: Gender, race, and class in reading methods. *Dissertation Abstracts International, 58*(07), 2509. (UMI No. 9802586)

Brown, E. (1993). In search of Nancy Drew, the Snow Queen, and Room Nineteen: Cruising for feminine discourse. *Frontiers, 13*(2), 1–25.

Duchein, M., & Konopak, B. (1994). *Women's reading and writing practices across the lifespan: Tree literary life histories.* Paper presented at the annual meeting of National Reading Conference, Charleston, SC.

Erickson, R., Otto, W., Randlett, A., Hayes, B., Cloer, T., Gustafson, D., & Smith, K. (1997). Looking for our literacy roots in all the right places. *Yearbook of the American Reading Forum, 209*–236.

Geissler, K.M. (1986). *The social meaning of women's literacy in nineteenth-century America.* Unpublished doctoral dissertation, University of Southern California.

Gritsavage, M. (1997, March). *Gender, culture, and literacy: Examining teacher's personal reflections and change by sex and age.* Paper presented at the annual meeting of the American Educational Research Association, Chicago, IL.

Guzzetti, B. (1997, March). *Gender, culture and literacy: Comparing students' reflections and change by demographics and ethnicity.* Paper presented at the annual meeting of the American Educational Research Association, Chicago, IL.

Hardenbrook, M.D. (1997, December). *Influences on reading in the development of literacies: Examining literacy autobiographies across the sexes.* Paper presented at the annual meeting of the National Reading Conference, Scottsdale, AZ.

Heath, S. (1989). Oral and literate traditions among black Americans living in poverty. *American Psychology, 44,* 367–373.

Jackson, D. (1989/1990). Patriarchy, class and language: A critical autobiography. *English in Education, 23/24,* 8–19.

Jackson, D. (1991). *Unmasking masculinity: A critical autobiography.* London: Unwin Hyman.

Luke, A., Cooke, S., & Luke, C. (1986). The selective tradition in action: Gender bias in student teachers' selections of children's literature. *English Education, 18*(4), 209–218.

Salvio, P.M. (1995). On the forbidden pleasures and hidden dangers of covert reading. *English Quarterly, 27*(3), 3–15.

Shannon, P. (1985). Reading instruction and social class. *Language Arts, 62*(6), 604–613.

Sohn, K.K. (1998, April). *Getting above their raisin's: Content analysis of literacy narratives.* Paper presented at the Annual Conference on College Composition and Communications, Chicago, IL.

Coding Form

Coding Sheet

I. Study's I.D. number:

II. Publication date of study:

III. First author's/researcher's name:
   1.

IV. Second author's/researcher's name:
   1.
   2. NA

V. Third author's/researcher's name:
   1.
   2. NA

VI. Additional authors/researchers?
   1. Yes
   2. No

VII. First author's ethnicity
   1. African American
   2. Asian
   3. European American
   4. Hispanic/Latina
   5. Native American
   6. Multiple ethnicities
   7. Other
   8. Unknown

VIII. First author's ethnicity
   1. Stated
   2. Inferred
   3. NA

IX. Second author's ethnicity
   1. African American
   2. Asian
   3. European American
   4. Hispanic/Latina
   5. Native American
   6. Multiple ethnicities
   7. Other
   8. Unknown
   9. NA

X. Second author's ethnicity
   1. Stated
   2. Inferred
   3. NA

XI. Third author's ethnicity
   1. African American
   2. Asian
   3. European American
   4. Hispanic/Latina
   5. Native American
   6. Multiple ethnicities
   7. Other
   8. Unknown
   9. NA

XII. Third author's ethnicity
   1. Stated
   2. Inferred
   3. NA

XIII. First author's gender
   1. Female
   2. Male
   3. Unknown

XIV. Second author's gender
   1. Female
   2. Male
   3. Unknown
   4. NA

XV. Third author's gender
   1. Female
   2. Male

      3. Unknown
      4. NA

XVI. Institutional affiliations of authors and researchers
      1. University/college
      2. Research & development center
      3. Public schools K–12
      4. Private schools K–12
      5. Preschool/day care
      6. Community agency
      7. University/school

XVII. Mode (major mode of literacy examined in study)
      1. Reading
      2. Discussion
      3. Writing
      4. Reading and writing
      5. Writing and discussion
      6. Reading and discussion
      7. Reading, writing, and discussion

XVIII. Type of study (how studies are sorted into folders)
      1. Reading
      2. Discussion
      3. Writing
      4. Canon (the classics)
      5. Autobiography
      6. School literary practices
      7. Introduction
      8. Textbooks, trade books, magazines, and tests
      9. Review of literature

XIX. Type of qualitative research
      1. Descriptive
      2. Mixed methods
      3. Qualitative
      4. Single-case study
      5. Multiple-case study
      6. Discourse analysis
      7. Teacher action research
      8. Ethnography
      9. Review
      10. Theoretical
      11. Combination (mixed methods)

12. Feminist qualitative
13. Life history

XX. Form
1. Book
2. Book chapter
3. ERIC document
4. Journal article (peer reviewed)
5. Journal article (not reviewed)
6. Unpublished paper/conference paper
7. Dissertation/thesis

XXI. Theoretical frameworks
1. Black feminism
2. Lesbian feminism
3. Radical feminism
4. Socialist feminism
5. Liberal feminism
6. Conservative feminism
7. Marxist feminism
8. Political feminism
9. Language as a social practice/sociolinguistics
10. Critical theory
11. Critical literacy
12. Critical feminism
13. Poststructural feminism
14. Literacy as a social practice
15. Social constructivism
16. Feminism not specified
17. Other
18. Not stated

XXII. Theoretical frameworks
1. Black feminism
2. Lesbian feminism
3. Radical feminism
4. Socialist feminism
5. Liberal feminism
6. Conservative feminism
7. Marxist feminism
8. Political feminism
9. Language as a social practice/sociolinguistics
10. Critical theory
11. Critical literacy

12. Critical feminism
13. Poststructural feminism
14. Literacy as a social practice
15. Social constructivism
16. Feminism not specified
17. Other
18. Not stated

XXIII. Theoretical frameworks
1. Black feminism
2. Lesbian feminism
3. Radical feminism
4. Socialist feminism
5. Liberal feminism
6. Conservative feminism
7. Marxist feminism
8. Political feminism
9. Language as a social practice/sociolinguistics
10. Critical theory
11. Critical literacy
12. Critical feminism
13. Poststructural feminism
14. Literacy as a social practice
15. Social constructivism
16. Feminism not specified
17. Other
18. Not stated

XXIV. Ethnicity or nationality of the majority of participants
1. African American
2. Asian American
3. European American
4. Hispanic/Latina
5. Native American
6. Unknown/Not Stated
7. Foreign born
8. Mexican
9. Other

XXV. Ethnicity or cultural group of the next largest group of participants
1. African American
2. Asian American
3. European American
4. Hispanic/Latina
5. Native American

6. Unknown/Not Stated
7. Foreign born
8. Other
9. NA

XXVI. Percentage of female participants
1. 100
2. 99–75
3. 74–50
4. 49–25
5. 24–1
6. Zero
7. Unknown

XXVII. Percentage of male participants
1. 100
2. 99–75
3. 74–50
4. 49–25
5. 24–1
6. Zero
7. Unknown

XXVIII. Grade level of participants
1. Preschool
2. Primary elementary
3. Intermediate elementary
4. Junior high school
5. Middle school
6. High school
7. Undergraduate student
8. Graduate student
9. Adult
10. Combination of grade levels

XXIX. Geographic location of study
1. United Kingdom
2. Western Europe
3. Eastern Europe
4. Canada
5. Caribbean
6. Central America
7. South America
8. United States
9. Australia
10. New Zealand

11. Africa
12. Far East
13. Middle East
14. Near East
15. Mexico

XXX. Context of study (learning environment)
1. Agencies/organizations
2. Community
3. Home
4. Public school K–8
5. Public school 9–12
6. Private school K–8
7. Private school 9–12
8. College or university
9. Home/school
10. University/school
11. University/home
12. University/agency
13. Agency/home
14. R & D center
15. Adult education
16. Combination of learning environments

XXXI. Socioeconomic status of participants
1. Working class
2. Working poor
3. Poverty level
4. Middle class
5. Upper middle class
6. Upper class
7. Other
8. Unknown

XXXII. Agency of participants
1. Active participants in research process
2. Passive participants in research process

XXXIII. First author's/researcher's role
1. Observer (interviewer/data collector)
2. Observer participant
3. Participant
4. Participant observer
5. Teacher research
6. Other
7. Unknown

XXXIV. Second author's/researcher's role
    1. Observer (interviewer; data collector)
    2. Observer participant
    3. Participant
    4. Participant observer
    5. Teacher research
    6. Unknown
    7. Other
    8. NA

XXXV. Third author's/researcher's role
    1. Observer (interviewer; data collector)
    2. Observer participant
    3. Participant observer
    4. Participant
    5. Teacher research
    6. Other
    7. Unknown
    8. NA

XXXVI. Does this article have a connection with other research?
    1. Yes
    2. No

_____

_____

Written comments

XXXVII. Researcher's assumption and frameworks

XXXVIII. Research questions or guiding question(s)

XXXIX. One paragraph summary of findings

XXXX. Most interesting (or major) finding of the study from our perspective

XXXXI. How does this article connect with other research?

XXXXII. Critique of the study
Where are the holes? From a perspective of social feminism—What was not said? What could we have looked at that we missed? Where are the silences? What does this study say about inequity that is caused by gender?

XXXXIII. Future directions
How could this study influence or stimulate social change? What can we infer from reading the study about social change and how literacy plays a role in this change? What can we infer about the interaction of social class, race, and gender and

literacy? What did we learn about literacy and gender from reading this study?

Add other questions to stimulate thinking about
1. literacy education
2. research

References

Acker, S. (1994, April). *Is research by a feminist always feminist research?* Paper presented at the annual meeting of the American Educational Research Association, New Orleans, LA.

Almasi, J. (1995). The nature of fourth-graders' sociocognitive conflicts in peer-led and teacher-led discussions of literature. *Reading Research Quarterly, 30,* 314–351.

Alvermann, D.E. (1986). Becoming a nation of readers: The report of the Commission on Reading—A critical review. *Georgia Journal of Reading, 1*(2), 24–27.

Alvermann, D.E. (1993, December). Student voice in class discussion: A feminist poststructuralist perspective. In D.E. Alvermann (Chair), *Expanding the possibilities: How feminist theories inform traditions and positions in reader response, classroom discussion, and critical thinking.* Symposium conducted at the annual meeting of the National Reading Conference, Charleston, SC.

Alvermann, D., & Anders, P. (1994, July). *New directions for inquiry and practice: Content area literacy from a feminist/critical perspective.* Paper presented at the International Reading Association's 15th World Congress on Reading, Buenos Aires, Argentina.

Alvermann, D.E., & Commeyras, M. (1994). *Gender, text, and discussion: Expanding the possibilities* (Perspectives in Reading Research Report No. 3). Athens, GA: National Reading Research Center.

Alvermann, D.E., Commeyras, M., Young, J.P., Randall, S., & Hinson, D. (1997). Interrupting gendered discursive practices in classroom talk about texts: Easy to think about, difficult to do. *Journal of Literacy Research, 29*(1), 73–104.

American Institutes for Research (1998). *Gender gaps: Where schools still fail our children.* Washington, DC: American Association of University Women.

Bardsley, D. (1999). *Boys and reading: What reading fiction means to sixth grade boys.* Unpublished doctoral dissertation, Arizona State University, Tempe.

Blair, H. (1996). *Gender and discourse: Adolescent girls construct gender through talk and text.* Unpublished doctoral dissertation, University of Arizona, Tucson. Also as Blair, H. (2000). Genderlects: Girl talk in a middle years language arts classroom. *Language Arts, 77*(2), 315–323.

Blake, B.E. (1997). *She say, he say! Urban girls write their lives.* Albany, NY: State University of New York Press.

Broughton, M.A. (1998). Early adolescent girls and their reading practices: Refection and transformation of subjectivities through experiences with literature (Doctoral dissertation, University of Georgia, 1998). *Dissertation Abstracts International, 59*(06), 1948. (AAT 9836306)

Brown, J. (1997). New heroes: Gender, race, fans and comic book superheroes (Doctoral dissertation, University of Toronto, Canada, 1998). *Dissertation Abstracts International, 59*(06), 1818. (AAT NQ27882)

Butler, J. (1990). *Gender trouble: Feminism and the subversion of identity.* New York: Routledge.

Carrington, K., & Bennett, A. (1996). "Girls'mags" and the pedagogical formation of the girl. In C. Luke (Ed.), *Feminisms and pedagogies of everyday life.* Albany, NY: State University of New York Press.

Cherland, M.R. (1992). Gendered readings: Cultured restraints upon response to literature. *The New Advocate, 5*(3), 187–197.

Cherland, M.R. (1994). *Private practices: Girls reading fiction and constructing identity.* London: Taylor & Francis.

Christian-Smith, L.K. (1993a). *Texts of desire: essays on fiction, femininity and schooling.* London; Washington, DC: Falmer Press.

Christian-Smith, L.K. (1993b). Voices of resistance: Young women readers of romance fiction. In L. Weis & M. Fine (Eds.), *Class, race, and gender in United States schools* (pp. 169–189). Albany, NY: State University of New York Press.

Christie, A. (1995). *No chips on their shoulders: Girls, boys and telecommunications.* Unpublished doctoral dissertation, Arizona State University, Tempe.

Cleary, L.M. (1996). "I think I know what my teachers want now": Gender and writing motivation. *English Journal, 85*(1), 50–57.

Dateline NBC. (1994). *Failing in fairness.* New York: National Broadcasting Company.

Davies, B. (1989). The discursive production of the male/female dualism in school settings. *Oxford Review of Education, 15*(3) 229–241.

Davies, B. (1993). *Shards of glass: Children reading and writing beyond gendered identities.* Cresskill, NJ: Hampton Press.

Davies, B. (1997). Constructing and deconstructing masculinities through critical literacy. *Gender and Education, 9*(1), 9–30.

146

Edelsky, C., & Harman, S. (1991). Risks and possibilities of whole language literacy: Alienation and connection. In C. Edelsky (Ed.), *With literacy and justice for all: Critical perspectives on literacy and education*. London: Falmer Press.

Enciso, P. (1998). Good/bad girls read together: Preadolescent girls' co-authorship of feminine subject positions during a shared reading event. *English Education, 30*, 44–66.

Erickson, F. (1985). *Qualitative methods in research on teaching* (Occasional Paper No. 81). Lansing, MI: Michigan State University, Institute for Research on Teaching.

Erickson, R., Otto, W., Randlett, A., Hayes, B., Cloer, T., Gustafson, D., & Smith, K. (1997). Looking for our literacy roots in all the right places. *Yearbook of the American Reading Forum, 209–236*.

Evans, K.S. (1999, April). Fifth-grade students' discussion groups. Paper presented at the annual meeting of the American Educational Research Association, Montreal, Canada.

Fey, M. (1997). Literate behavior in a cross-age computer-mediated discussion: A question of empowerment. In C. Kinzer, K. Hinchman, & D. Leu (Eds.), *Inquiries in literacy theory and practice: Forty-sixth yearbook of the National Reading Conference* (pp. 507–518). Chicago: National Reading Conference.

Fey, M. (1998). Critical literacy in school-college collaboration through computer networking: A feminist research project. *Journal of Literacy Research, 30*(1), 85–117.

Fordham, S. (1993). Those loud Black girls: (Black) women, silence, and gender "passing" in the academy. *Anthropology and Education Quarterly, 24*(1), 3–32.

Fyfe, L.M. (1999). The role of gender in the writing of primary school children. Unpublished manuscript, Arizona State University, Tempe.

Gallas, K. (1995). *Talking their way into science: Hearing children's questions and theories, responding with curricula*. New York: Teachers College Press.

Gerver, E., & Lewis, L. (1984). Women, computers, and adult education: Liberation or oppression? *Convergence: An International Journal of Adult Education, 17*(4), 5–16.

Gilbert, P. (1983). Down among the women: Girls as readers and writers. *English in Australia, 64*, 26–29.

Gilbert, P. (1992). The story so far: Gender, literacy and social regulation. *Gender and Education, 4*(3), 185–199.

Gilligan, C. (1982). *In a different voice: Psychological theory and women's development*. Cambridge, MA: Harvard University Press.

Giroux, H.A. (1995). Language, difference, and curriculum theory: Beyond the politics of clarity. In P.L. McLaren & J.M. Giarelli (Eds.), *Critical theory and educational research* (pp. 23–28). New York: State University of New York Press.

Glaser, B.G., & Strauss, A.C. (1967). *The discovery of grounded theory.* Chicago: Aldine.

Goffman, E. (1977). The arrangement between the sexes. *Theory and Society, 4,* 301–331.

Gore, J. (1993). *The struggle for pedagogies.* New York; London: Routledge.

Grant, C.A., & Sleeter, C.E. (1986). Race, class and gender in education research: An argument for integrative analysis. *Review of Educational Research, 56*(2),195–211.

Graves, D. (1975). An examination of the writing process of seven-year-old children. *Research in the Teaching of English, 9*(3), 227–241.

Gray, J. (1997). *Mars and Venus on a date.* New York: HarperCollins.

Gritsavage, M. (1997a). *Examining dominance in discourse in the graduate course, Gender, Culture and Literacy.* Unpublished manuscript, Arizona State University, Tempe.

Gritsavage, M. (1997b, December). *Gendered discourse in classroom conversations about gender, culture, and literacy.* Paper presented at the annual meeting of the National Reading Conference, Scottsdale, AZ.

Guzzetti, B. (1997, March). *Gender, culture and literacy: Comparing students' reflections and change by demographics and ethnicity.* Paper presented at the annual meeting of the American Educational Research Association, Chicago, IL.

Guzzetti, B. (2001). Texts and talk: The role of gender in learning physics. In E.B. Moje & D. O'Brien (Eds.), *Constructions of literacy: Studies of teaching and learning literacy in secondary classrooms* (pp. 125–146) Mahwah, NJ: Erlbaum.

Guzzetti, B.J., & Williams, W.O. (1996a). Changing the pattern of gendered discussion: Lessons from science classrooms. *Journal of Adolescent & Adult Literacy, 40,* 2–11.

Guzzetti, B.J., & Williams, W.O. (1996b). Gender, text, and discussion: Examining intellectual safety in the science classroom. *Journal of Research in Science Teaching, 33*(1), 5–20.

Haag, P. (1999). *Voices of a generation: Teenage girls on sex, school and self.* Washington, DC: American Association of University Women.

Hall, R.M., & Sandler, B.R. (1982). The classroom climate: A chilly one for women? (Project on the Status and Education of Women). Washington, DC: Association of American Colleges.

Hardenbrook, M.D. (1997, December). *Influences on reading in the development of literacies: Examining literacy autobiographies across the sexes.* Paper presented at the annual meeting of the National Reading Conference, Scottsdale, AZ.

Henkin, R. (1995). Insiders and outsiders in first-grade writing workshops: Gender and equity issues. *Language Arts, 72*, 429–434.

Hsi, S., & Hoadley, C.M. (1997). Productive discussion in science: Gender equity through electronic discourse. *Journal of Science Education and Technology, 4*(1), 23–36.

Hunt, S. (1995). Choice in the writing class: How do students decide what to write and how to write it? *The Quarterly of the National Writing Project and the Center for the Study of Writing, 17*(2), 7–11.

Jackson, D. (1989/1990). Patriarchy, class and language: A critical autobiography. *English in Education, 23/24*, 8–19.

Jackson, G. (1980). Methods for integative reviews. *Review of Educational Research, 50*(3), 438–460.

Jones, M.G., & Wheatley, J. (1990). Gender differences in teacher-student interactions in science classrooms. *Journal of Research in Science Teaching, 27*, 861–874.

Jungvarth, H. (1991). Interaction and gender: Findings of a microethnography approach to classroom discourse. *Educational Studies in Mathematics, 22*, 263–284.

Kahle, J.B., & Rennie, L.J. (1993). Ameliorating gender differences in attitudes about science. A cross-national study. *Journal of Science Education and Technology, 2*(1), 321–324.

Kamler, B. (1994). Gender and genre in early writing. *Linguistics and Education, 6*, 153–182.

Kamler, B. (1999, November). *Using critical literacy to develop new classroom writing practices.* Paper presented at the annual meeting of the National Council of Teachers of English, Denver, CO.

Kingston Friends Workshop Group. (1985). *Ways and means: An approach to problem solving.* Kingston, UK: Society of Friends.

Lakoff, R. (1975). *Language and women's place.* New York: Harper Row

Lankshear, C., & McLaren, P.L. (Eds.) (1993). *Critical literacy: Politics, praxis, and the postmodern.* Albany, NY: State University of New York Press.

Lewis, C., & Fabos, B. (1999, December). *Chatting on-line: Uses of instant message communication among adolescent girls.* Paper presented at the annual meeting of the National Reading Conference, Orlando, FL.

Luce-Kapler, R. (1999). As if women writing. *Journal of Literacy Research, 31*, 267–291.

Lytle, S., & Cochran-Smith, M. (1992). Teacher research as a way of knowing. *Harvard Educational Review, 62*, 447–474.

MacGillivray, L., & Martinez, A.M. (1998). Princesses who commit suicide: Primary children writing within and against gender stereotypes. *Journal of Literacy Research, 30*(1), 53–84.

Many, J.E. (1989) Sex roles from a child's point of view: An analysis of children's writing. *Reading Psychology, 10*(4), 357–370.

149

McConnell, D. (1997). Interaction patterns of mixed sex groups in educational computer conferences, Part I—Empirical findings. *Gender and Education, 9*(3), 343–363.

Miles, M.B., & Huberman, A.M. (1984). *Qualitative data analysis: A sourcebook of new methods.* Thousand Oaks, CA: Sage.

Nelson, K.A. (1990). Gender communication through small groups. *English Journal,* 58–61.

Nielsen, L. (1994). *You shouldn't have to bring your Dad.* Paper presented at the annual meeting of the National Reading Conference, Charleston, SC.

Nielsen, L. (1998). Coding the light: Rethinking generational authority in a rural high school telecommunications project. In D. Reinking & L. Labbo (Eds.), *Handbook of literacy and technology: Transformations in a post-typographical world.* Mahwah, NJ: Erlbaum.

Orellana, M.F. (1995). Literacy as a gendered social practice: Tasks, texts, talk and take up. *Reading Research Quarterly, 30,* 674–708.

Osmont, P. (1987). Teacher inquiry in the classroom: Reading and gender set. *Language Arts, 64*(7), 758–761.

Peterson, S. (1998). Evaluation and teachers' perceptions of gender in sixth-grade student writing. *Research in the Teaching of English, 33,* 181–208.

Reed, L.R. (1999). Troubling boys and disturbing discourses on masculinity and schooling: A feminist exploration of current debates and interventions concerning boys in school. *Gender and Education, 11*(1), 93–110.

Rosenblatt, L. (1985) The transactional theory of the literary work: Implications for research. In C. Cooper (Ed.), *Researching response to literature and the teaching of literature.* Norwood, NJ: Ablex.

Sadker, M., & Sadker, D. (1994). *Failing in fairness: How America's schools cheat girls.* New York: Scribners.

Siegel, M. (1989). A critical review of reading in mathematics instruction: The need for a new synthesis. (ERIC Document Reproduction Service No. ED 301863)

Smith, M.L., & Glass, G.V (1987). *Research and evaluation in education and the social sciences.* New York: Prentice Hall.

Sohn, K.K. (1998, April). *Getting above their raisin's: Content analysis of literacy narratives.* Paper presented at the Annual Conference on College Composition and Communications, Chicago, IL.

Solsken, J. (1993). *Literacy, gender and work in families and in school.* Norwood, NJ: Ablex.

Spender, D. (1995). *Nattering on the net: Women, power and cyberspace.* North Melbourne, Victoria, Australia: Spinifex Press.

Stake, R. (1994). Case studies. In N.K. Denzin & Y.S. Lincoln (Eds.), *Handbook of qualitative research: A sourcebook of new methods.* Thousand Oaks, CA: Sage.

Stanley, L., & Wise, S. (1993). *Breaking out again: Feminist ontology and epistemology*. London: Routledge.

Swisshelm, J.G. (1880). *Half a century*. Chicago: unknown.

Tobin, K. (1988). Differential engagement of males and females in high school science. *International Journal of Science Education, 10*, 441–456.

Trepanier-Street, M.L., & Ramatowski, J.A. (1999). The influence of gender role perceptions: A re-examination. *Early Childhood Education, 26*(3), 155–159.

Tromel-Plotz, S. (1985). *Women's conversational culture: Rupturing patriarchal discourse*. Rolig Paper 36, Roskilde Universssitetscenter, Roskilde, Denmark.

Vygotsky, L.S. (1978). *Mind in society: The development of higher psychological processes* (M. Cole, V. John-Steiner, S. Scribner, & E. Souberman, Eds. and Trans.). Cambridge, MA: Harvard University Press. (Original work published 1934)

West, C., & Zimmermann, D. (1987). Doing gender. *Gender and Society, 1*, 151

Winterson, J. (1995). *Art objects*. Toronto, ON: Knopf.

Young, J.P. (2000). Boy talk: Critical literacies and masculinities. *Reading Research Quarterly, 35*, 312–337.

Literature References

Alexander, L. (1999). *The book of three*. New York: Henry Holt.

Babbitt, N. (1986). *Tuck everlasting*. New York: Farrar, Straus & Giroux.

Beatty, P. (1981). *Lupita manana*. New York: HarperCollins.

Browne, A. (1986). *Piggybook*. New York: Random Library.

Burnett, F.H. (1987). *The secret garden*. New York: HarperCollins.

Byars, B. (1996). *Summer of the swans*. New York: Viking.

Craighead, J.C. (1972). *Julie of the wolves*. New York: Harper.

Fine, A. (1991). *Bill's new frock*. Bath, UK: Chivers.

Morrison, T. (1987). *Song of Solomon*. New York: Plume.

O'Dell, S. (1990). *Island of the Blue Dolphins*. Boston: Houghton Mifflin.

Paterson, K. (1980). *Jacob have I loved*. New York: Crowell.

Peck, R. (1989). I go along. In D. Gallo (Ed.), *Connections: Short stories by outstanding writers for young adults* (pp. 184–191). New York: Dell

Pfeffer, S.B. (1977). *Kid power*. New York: Scholastic.

Schaefer, J. (1981). *Shane*. New York: Bantam.

Shakespeare, W. (1998). *Hamlet*. New York: Oxford University Press.

Taylor, M.D. (1997). *Roll of thunder, hear my cry*. New York: Puffin.

Author Index

A

Acker, S., 43
Almasi, J., 39
Alvermann, D.E., 3, 5, 7, 9, 17, 19–20, 21–22, 28, 31, 34–35, 36, 42, 97
American Institutes for Research, 4
Anders, P.L., 9, 17, 21–22, 31, 36

B

Bardsley, D., 5, 64–65
Barrow, I., 46, 49
Bassard, K.C., 113
Beach, R., 65, 67
Benjamin, B., 55, 58
Bennett, A., 9
Berger-Knorr, A., 108
Blair, H., 51, 55–57, 66, 84–86, 93, 118
Blake, B.E., 86–87, 119
Broaddus, K., 46, 49
Brodkey, L., 82
Broughton, M.A., 5, 46, 55
Brown, E., 107–108
Brown, J., 5, 55, 62–63
Brown, V.A., 80–81
Burdick, T., 82–83
Butler, J., 8

C

Carrington, K., 9
Cherland, M.R., 2, 5, 20, 46–48, 55, 58, 60–61, 69–72, 76, 78, 118
Chiang, C., 28–29

Y

Z

Subject Index

A

INSTRUCTION: memories of, gender and, 55–57; oppression/constraint in, 64–69; recommendations for, 41–42, 75–77, 92–93, 103, 115, 119

L

LANGUAGE PATTERNS, 17–19; examples of, 1–2
LIFE MARKERS/STAGES: and literacy autobiography, 112–113
LITERACY AUTOBIOGRAPHY, 105–116; recommendations for, 115–116
LITERACY DEVELOPMENT: gendered and social nature of, 106–109; memories of, gender and, 55–57; multiple subjectivities and, 111–113; potentials and limits of, 113–114; social repercussions of, 109–111
LITERARY FORMS: experimentation with, 87, 92–93
LITERATURE RESPONSE: gendered talk in, 19–28; text and method and, 46–55
LITERATURE REVIEW: coding form used for, 12, 136–144; limitations of, 9–10; organization of, 14; principles of, 7–8; procedures in, 10–14; purpose of, 6–7

M

MAGAZINES, 58, 61–62
MALES: discomfort with gender discussions, 33; language patterns of, 1–2; reader responses of, 47
MARGINALIZATION, 118
MIXED-GENDER GROUPS, 19–28; electronic text use by, 98–99
MULTIPLE SUBJECTIVITIES: and literacy development, 111–113

N

NANCY DREW MYSTERIES, 71, 108
NOTE WRITING, 80–81

O

OPPOSITION: in reading, 69–72
OPPRESSION, 118; in instructional and social context, 64–69

P

PARENTS: and literacy development, 109–111; and reading practices, 65–66; and writing practices, 85
PEER REACTION: and gendered writing practices, 83–84
POWER RELATIONS: and discourse, 31, 33; electronic text and, 98

R

READER RESPONSE: gendered talk in, 19–28; text and method and, 46–55

READING, 45–78; recommendations for, 75–78

READING PREFERENCES/PRACTICES: gendered, 55–64

RECIPROCAL TALK, 30

RESEARCH: recommendations for, 42–44, 77–78, 93–94, 103–104, 116, 120–122

RESISTANCE: to assigned texts, 59; in reading, 69–72

RESPECT ISSUES, 24

ROMANCE NOVELS, 58–60, 72, 109–110

S

SEX. *See* gender

SILENCE: as participation, 36

SILENCING OF FEMALES: electronic text and, 98–102; instructional context and, 68–69; language patterns in, 17–19; in literature-response groups, 21–23; in reader-response groups, 50

SINGLE-GENDER GROUPS: electronic text use by, 98–99; for literature response, 26–27; recommendations for, 42, 119; for writing, 86–89

SITES OF POSSIBILITIES: gendered writing practices in, 86–89

SOCIAL CONTEXT: and literacy development, 106–109; and reading, 64–69; and writing, 80–84

SOCIAL RELATIONSHIPS: electronic text and, 96–98

SOCIOECONOMIC STATUS, in studies, 117

SPORTS: versus reading, 65–66

STORYTELLING, 27

SUBJECTIVITIES: multiple, and literacy development, 111–113

T

TEASING, 20–21

TESTIFYING, 27

THEMES, 118; in discussion studies, 16; in electronic text studies, 95–96; in reading studies, 46; in writing studies, 80

TOPIC CHOICE, 5–6, 82–83, 86

W

WRITING, 79–94; as gendered social practice, 80–84; recommendations for, 92–94